International Monetary
Arrangements
for the 21st Century

Integrating National Economies: Promise and Pitfalls

Barry Bosworth (Brookings Institution) and Gur Ofer (Hebrew University)
Reforming Planned Economies in an Integrating World Economy

Ralph C. Bryant (Brookings Institution)
International Coordination of National Stabilization Policies

Susan M. Collins (Brookings Institution/Georgetown University)
Distributive Issues: A Constraint on Global Integration

Richard N. Cooper (Harvard University)
Environment and Resource Policies for the World Economy

Ronald G. Ehrenberg (Cornell University)
Labor Markets and Integrating National Economies

Barry Eichengreen (University of California, Berkeley)
International Monetary Arrangements for the 21st Century

Mitsuhiro Fukao (Bank of Japan)
Financial Integration, Corporate Governance, and the Performance of Multinational Companies

Stephan Haggard (University of California, San Diego)
Developing Nations and the Politics of Global Integration

Richard J. Herring (University of Pennsylvania) and Robert E. Litan (Department of Justice/Brookings Institution)
Financial Regulation in the Global Economy

Miles Kahler (University of California, San Diego)
International Institutions and the Political Economy of Integration

Anne O. Krueger (Stanford University)
Trade Policies and Developing Nations

Robert Z. Lawrence (Harvard University)
Regionalism, Multilateralism, and Deeper Integration

Sylvia Ostry (University of Toronto) and Richard R. Nelson (Columbia University)
Techno-Nationalism and Techno-Globalism: Conflict and Cooperation

Robert L. Paarlberg (Wellesley College/Harvard University)
Leadership Abroad Begins at Home: U.S. Foreign Economic Policy after the Cold War

Peter Rutland (Wesleyan University)
Russia, Eurasia, and the Global Economy

F. M. Scherer (Harvard University)
Competition Policies for an Integrated World Economy

Susan L. Shirk (University of California, San Diego)
How China Opened Its Door: The Political Success of the PRC's Foreign Trade and Investment Reforms

Alan O. Sykes (University of Chicago)
Product Standards for Internationally Integrated Goods Markets

Akihiko Tanaka (Institute of Oriental Culture, University of Tokyo)
The Politics of Deeper Integration: National Attitudes and Policies in Japan

Vito Tanzi (International Monetary Fund)
Taxation in an Integrating World

William Wallace (St. Antony's College, Oxford University)
Regional Integration: The West European Experience

Barry Eichengreen

International Monetary Arrangements for the 21st Century

THE BROOKINGS INSTITUTION
Washington, D.C.

Library of Congress Cataloging-in-Publication data:
Barry Eichengreen
International monetary arrangements for the 21st century/Barry Eichengreen
p. cm. — (Integrating national economies)
Includes bibliographical references and index.
ISBN 0-8157-2276-1 (cloth) — ISBN 0-8157-2275-3 (paper)
1. Foreign exchange—Government policy. 2. Monetary policy.
3. International finance. I. Title. II. Series.
HG3851.E33 1994
332.4'5—dc20   94-23163
                                                                CIP

9 8 7 6 5 4 3 2 1

The paper used in this publication meets the minimum requirements of
American National Standard for Information Sciences—Permanence of Paper
for Printed Library Materials, ANSI Z39.48-1984

Typeset in Plantin

Composition by Princeton Editorial Associates
Princeton, New Jersey

Printed by R. R. Donnelley and Sons Co.
Harrisonburg, Virginia

The Brookings Institution is an independent organization devoted to nonpartisan research, education, and publication in economics, government, foreign policy, and the social sciences generally. Its principal purposes are to aid in the development of sound public policies and to promote public understanding of issues of national importance.

The Institution was founded on December 8, 1927, to merge the activities of the Institute for Government Research, founded in 1916, the Institute of Economics, founded in 1922, and the Robert Brookings Graduate School of Economics and Government, founded in 1924.

The Board of Trustees is responsible for the general administration of the Institution, while the immediate direction of the policies, program, and staff is vested in the President, assisted by an advisory committee of the officers and staff. The by-laws of the Institution state: "It is the function of the Trustees to make possible the conduct of scientific research, and publication, under the most favorable conditions, and to safeguard the independence of the research staff in the pursuit of their studies and in the publication of the results of such studies. It is not a part of their function to determine, control, or influence the conduct of particular investigations or the conclusions reached."

The President bears final responsibility for the decision to publish a manuscript as a Brookings book. In reaching his judgment on the competence, accuracy, and objectivity of each study, the President is advised by the director of the appropriate research program and weighs the views of a panel of expert outside readers who report to him in confidence on the quality of the work. Publication of a work signifies that it is deemed a competent treatment worthy of public consideration but does not imply endorsement of conclusions or recommendations.

The Institution maintains its position of neutrality on issues of public policy in order to safeguard the intellectual freedom of the staff. Hence interpretations or conclusions in Brookings publications should be understood to be solely those of the authors and should not be attributed to the Institution, to its trustees, officers, or other staff members, or to the organizations that support its research.

Foreword

THE 1990s have been turbulent times for the international monetary system. In 1992 a series of speculative crises battered the Exchange Rate Mechanism of the European Monetary System (EMS), forcing Italy and the United Kingdom to withdraw. The Scandinavian countries were forced to abandon the exchange rate pegs that they had established over the course of previous years. In 1993 the crisis spread to other European currencies, forcing Europe to relinquish the narrow bands of the EMS for a much more permissive system. In the summer of 1994, the U.S. dollar depreciated sharply against the Japanese yen, deepening policymakers' dissatisfaction with floating exchange rates among the major currencies. Coming as they did, on the eve of the fiftieth anniversary of the Bretton Woods Agreement, these events did much to rekindle the debate over the future of the international monetary system.

In this book, Barry Eichengreen analyzes international monetary options for the twenty-first century. He argues that it will not be possible for governments to prevent exchange rate movements from exceeding prespecified limits. If this conclusion is correct, it rules out the sustainability of pegged but adjustable exchange rates, crawling pegs, and other regimes in which governments preannounce limits for exchange rate fluctuations. Countries that have traditionally pegged their currencies will be forced to choose between floating exchange rates and monetary unification.

Barry Eichengreen is John L. Simpson Professor of Economics and Professor of Political Science at the University of California at Berkeley. He gratefully acknowledges the assistance of Brian A'Hearn and

Lisa Ortiz in researching this manuscript, and Pamela Fox's help in processing it. Portions of the study were undertaken during visits to the Institute for Advanced Study in Berlin, the Institute for International Economic Studies in Stockholm, and the International Monetary Fund. Helpful comments were provided by Michael Bordo, Ralph Bryant, Benjamin Cohen, Max Corden, Andrew Crockett, Jeff Frankel, Jeff Frieden, Hans Genberg, Alberto Giovannini, Lars Jonung, Peter Kenen, Jacques Melitz, Maury Obstfeld, Lars Svensson, and John Williamson. The author is especially indebted to Maury Obstfeld, on whose theoretical work the manuscript draws, and to Charles Wyplosz for several years of collaboration on these issues.

At Brookings Laura Kelly and Kathleen McDill verified the manuscript. Princeton Editorial Associates edited it and prepared the index.

Funding for the project came from the Center for Global Partnership of the Japan Foundation, the Curry Foundation, the Ford Foundation, the Korea Foundation, the Tokyo Club Foundation for Global Studies, the United States-Japan Foundation, and the Alex C. Walker Educational and Charitable Foundation. The author and Brookings are grateful for their support.

The views expressed in this book are those of the author and should not be ascribed to the persons or organizations whose assistance is acknowledged or to the trustees, officers, or staff members of the Brookings Institution.

BRUCE K. MACLAURY
President

September 1994
Washington, D.C.

In truth, the free movement of capital is incompatible with a system of exchange rates that are occasionally changed by consequential amounts and in a predictable direction. . . . These various considerations lead me to conclude that we will need a system of credibly fixed exchange rates. . . . if we are to preserve an open trading and financial system. Exchange rates can be most credibly fixed if they are eliminated altogether, that is, if international transactions take place with a single currency.

Richard Cooper

Contents

Figures

Preface to the Studies on Integrating National Economies

*E*CONOMIC interdependence among nations has increased sharply in the past half century. For example, while the value of total production of industrial countries increased at a rate of about 9 percent a year on average between 1964 and 1992, the value of the exports of those nations grew at an average rate of 12 percent, and lending and borrowing across national borders through banks surged upward even more rapidly at 23 percent a year. This international economic interdependence has contributed to significantly improved standards of living for most countries. Continuing international economic integration holds out the promise of further benefits. Yet the increasing sensitivity of national economies to events and policies originating abroad creates dilemmas and pitfalls if national policies and international cooperation are poorly managed.

The Brookings Project on Integrating National Economies, of which this study is a component, focuses on the interplay between two fundamental facts about the world at the end of the twentieth century. First, the world will continue for the foreseeable future to be organized politically into nation-states with sovereign governments. Second, increasing economic integration among nations will continue to erode differences among national economies and undermine the autonomy of national governments. The project explores the opportunities and tensions arising from these two facts.

Scholars from a variety of disciplines have produced twenty-one studies for the first phase of the project. Each study examines the heightened competition between national political sovereignty and increased cross-border economic integration. This preface identifies background themes and issues common to all the studies and provides a brief overview of the project as a whole.[1]

Increasing World Economic Integration

Two underlying sets of causes have led nations to become more closely intertwined. First, technological, social, and cultural changes have sharply reduced the effective economic distances among nations. Second, many of the government policies that traditionally inhibited cross-border transactions have been relaxed or even dismantled.

The same improvements in transportation and communications technology that make it much easier and cheaper for companies in New York to ship goods to California, for residents of Strasbourg to visit relatives in Marseilles, and for investors in Hokkaido to buy and sell shares on the Tokyo Stock Exchange facilitate trade, migration, and capital movements spanning nations and continents. The sharply reduced costs of moving goods, money, people, and information underlie the profound economic truth that technology has made the world markedly smaller.

New communications technology has been especially significant for financial activity. Computers, switching devices, and telecommunications satellites have slashed the cost of transmitting information internationally, of confirming transactions, and of paying for transactions. In the 1950s, for example, foreign exchange could be bought and sold only during conventional business hours in the initiating party's time zone. Such transactions can now be carried out instantaneously twenty-four hours a day. Large banks pass the management of their worldwide foreign-exchange positions around the globe from one branch to another, staying continuously ahead of the setting sun.

Such technological innovations have increased the knowledge of potentially profitable international exchanges and of economic opportunities abroad. Those developments, in turn, have changed consumers' and producers' tastes. Foreign goods, foreign vacations, foreign financial investments—virtually anything from other nations—have lost some of their exotic character.

1. A complete list of authors and study titles is included at the beginning of this volume, facing the title page.

Although technological change permits increased contact among nations, it would not have produced such dramatic effects if it had been countermanded by government policies. Governments have traditionally taxed goods moving in international trade, directly restricted imports and subsidized exports, and tried to limit international capital movements. Those policies erected "separation fences" at the borders of nations. From the perspective of private sector agents, separation fences imposed extra costs on cross-border transactions. They reduced trade and, in some cases, eliminated it. During the 1930s governments used such policies with particular zeal, a practice now believed to have deepened and lengthened the Great Depression.

After World War II, most national governments began—sometimes unilaterally, more often collaboratively—to lower their separation fences, to make them more permeable, or sometimes even to tear down parts of them. The multilateral negotiations under the auspices of the General Agreement on Trade and Tariffs (GATT)—for example, the Kennedy Round in the 1960s, the Tokyo Round in the 1970s, and most recently the protracted negotiations of the Uruguay Round, formally signed only in April 1994—stand out as the most prominent examples of fence lowering for trade in goods. Though contentious and marked by many compromises, the GATT negotiations are responsible for sharp reductions in at-the-border restrictions on trade in goods and services. After the mid-1980s a large number of developing countries moved unilaterally to reduce border barriers and to pursue outwardly oriented policies.

The lowering of fences for financial transactions began later and was less dramatic. Nonetheless, by the 1990s government restrictions on capital flows, especially among the industrial countries, were much less important and widespread than at the end of World War II and in the 1950s.

By shrinking the economic distances among nations, changes in technology would have progressively integrated the world economy even in the absence of reductions in governments' separation fences. Reductions in separation fences would have enhanced interdependence even without the technological innovations. Together, these two sets of evolutionary changes have reinforced each other and strikingly transformed the world economy.

Changes in the Government of Nations

Simultaneously with the transformation of the global economy, major changes have occurred in the world's political structure. First, the number of governmental decisionmaking units in the world has expanded markedly and political power has been diffused more broadly among them. Rising nationalism and, in some areas, heightened ethnic tensions have accompanied that increasing political pluralism.

The history of membership in international organizations documents the sharp growth in the number of independent states. For example, only 44 nations participated in the Bretton Woods conference of July 1944, which gave birth to the International Monetary Fund. But by the end of 1970, the IMF had 118 member nations. The number of members grew to 150 by the mid-1980s and to 178 by December 1993. Much of this growth reflects the collapse of colonial empires. Although many nations today are small and carry little individual weight in the global economy, their combined influence is considerable and their interests cannot be ignored as easily as they were in the past.

A second political trend, less visible but equally important, has been the gradual loss of the political and economic hegemony of the United States. Immediately after World War II, the United States by itself accounted for more than one-third of world production. By the early 1990s the U.S. share had fallen to about one-fifth. Concurrently, the political and economic influence of the European colonial powers continued to wane, and the economic significance of nations outside Europe and North America, such as Japan, Korea, Indonesia, China, Brazil, and Mexico, increased. A world in which economic power and influence are widely diffused has displaced a world in which one or a few nations effectively dominated international decisionmaking.

Turmoil and the prospect of fundamental change in the formerly centrally planned economies compose a third factor causing radical changes in world politics. During the era of central planning, governments in those nations tried to limit external influences on their economies. Now leaders in the formerly planned economies are trying to adopt reforms modeled on Western capitalist principles. To the extent that these efforts succeed, those nations will increase their economic involvement with the rest of the world. Political and economic alignments among the Western industrialized nations will be forced to adapt.

Governments and scholars have begun to assess these three trends, but their far-reaching ramifications will not be clear for decades.

Dilemmas for National Policies

Cross-border economic integration and national political sovereignty have increasingly come into conflict, leading to a growing mismatch between the economic and political structures of the world. The effective domains of economic markets have come to coincide less and less with national governmental jurisdictions.

When the separation fences at nations' borders were high, governments and citizens could sharply distinguish "international" from "domestic" policies. International policies dealt with at-the-border barriers, such as tariffs and quotas, or responded to events occurring abroad. In contrast, domestic policies were concerned with everything behind the nation's borders, such as competition and antitrust rules, corporate governance, product standards, worker safety, regulation and supervision of financial institutions, environmental protection, tax codes, and the government's budget. Domestic policies were regarded as matters about which nations were sovereign, to be determined by the preferences of the nation's citizens and its political institutions, without regard for effects on other nations.

As separation fences have been lowered and technological innovations have shrunk economic distances, a multitude of formerly neglected differences among nations' domestic policies have become exposed to international scrutiny. National governments and international negotiations must thus increasingly deal with "deeper"— behind-the-border—integration. For example, if country A permits companies to emit air and water pollutants whereas country B does not, companies that use pollution-generating methods of production will find it cheaper to produce in country A. Companies in country B that compete internationally with companies in country A are likely to complain that foreign competitors enjoy unfair advantages and to press for international pollution standards.

Deeper integration requires analysis of the economic and the political aspects of virtually all nonborder policies and practices. Such

issues have already figured prominently in negotiations over the evolution of the European Community, over the Uruguay Round of
GATT negotiations, over the North American Free Trade Agreement
(NAFTA), and over the bilateral economic relationships between
Japan and the United States. Future debates about behind-the-border
policies will occur with increasing frequency and prove at least as
complex and contentious as the past negotiations regarding at-the-
border restrictions.

Tensions about deeper integration arise from three broad sources:
cross-border spillovers, diminished national autonomy, and challenges
to political sovereignty.

Cross-Border Spillovers

Some activities in one nation produce consequences that spill
across borders and affect other nations. Illustrations of these spillovers abound. Given the impact of modern technology of banking
and securities markets in creating interconnected networks, lax rules
in one nation erode the ability of all other nations to enforce banking
and securities rules and to deal with fraudulent transactions. Given
the rapid diffusion of knowledge, science and technology policies in
one nation generate knowledge that other nations can use without full
payment. Labor market policies become matters of concern to other
nations because workers migrate in search of work; policies in one
nation can trigger migration that floods or starves labor markets
elsewhere. When one nation dumps pollutants into the air or water
that other nations breathe or drink, the matter goes beyond the
unitary concern of the polluting nation and becomes a matter for
international negotiation. Indeed, the hydrocarbons that are emitted
into the atmosphere when individual nations burn coal for generating
electricity contribute to global warming and are thereby a matter of
concern for the entire world.

The tensions associated with cross-border spillovers can be especially vexing when national policies generate outcomes alleged to be
competitively inequitable, as in the example in which country A
permits companies to emit pollutants and country B does not. Or
consider a situation in which country C requires commodities, whether
produced at home or abroad, to meet certain design standards, justified for safety reasons. Foreign competitors may find it too expensive

to meet these standards. In that event, the standards in C act very much like tariffs or quotas, effectively narrowing or even eliminating foreign competition for domestic producers. Citing examples of this sort, producers or governments in individual nations often complain that business is not conducted on a "level playing field." Typically, the complaining nation proposes that *other* nations adjust their policies to moderate or remove the competitive inequities.

Arguments for creating a level playing field are troublesome at best. International trade occurs precisely because of differences among nations—in resource endowments, labor skills, and consumer tastes. Nations specialize in producing goods and services in which they are relatively most efficient. In a fundamental sense, cross-border trade is valuable because the playing field is *not* level.

When David Ricardo first developed the theory of comparative advantage, he focused on differences among nations owing to climate or technology. But Ricardo could as easily have ascribed the productive differences to differing "social climates" as to physical or technological climates. Taking all "climatic" differences as given, the theory of comparative advantage argues that free trade among nations will maximize global welfare.

Taken to its logical extreme, the notion of leveling the playing field implies that nations should become homogeneous in all major respects. But that recommendation is unrealistic and even pernicious. Suppose country A decides that it is too poor to afford the costs of a clean environment, and will thus permit the production of goods that pollute local air and water supplies. Or suppose it concludes that it cannot afford stringent protections for worker safety. Country A will then argue that it is inappropriate for other nations to impute to country A the value they themselves place on a clean environment and safety standards (just as it would be inappropriate to impute the A valuations to the environment of other nations). The core of the idea of political sovereignty is to permit national residents to order their lives and property in accord with their own preferences.

Which perspective about differences among nations in behind-the-border policies is more compelling? Is country A merely exercising its national preferences and appropriately exploiting its comparative advantage in goods that are dirty or dangerous to produce? Or does a legitimate international problem exist that justifies pressure from other nations urging country A to accept changes in its policies (thus curbing its national sovereignty)? When national governments negotiate resolutions to such questions—trying to agree whether individual nations are legitimately exercising sovereign choices or, alternatively, engaging in behavior that is unfair or damaging to other nations—the dialogue is invariably contentious because the resolutions depend on the typically complex circumstances of the international spillovers and on the relative weights accorded to the interests of particular individuals and particular nations.

Diminished National Autonomy

As cross-border economic integration increases, governments experience greater difficulties in trying to control events within their borders. Those difficulties, summarized by the term *diminished autonomy*, are the second set of reasons why tensions arise from the competition between political sovereignty and economic integration.

For example, nations adjust monetary and fiscal policies to influence domestic inflation and employment. In setting these policies, smaller countries have always been somewhat constrained by foreign economic events and policies. Today, however, all nations are constrained, often severely. More than in the past, therefore, nations may be better able to achieve their economic goals if they work together collaboratively in adjusting their macroeconomic policies.

Diminished autonomy and cross-border spillovers can sometimes be allowed to persist without explicit international cooperation to deal with them. States in the United States adopt their own tax systems and set policies for assistance to poor single people without any formal cooperation or limitation. Market pressures operate to force a degree of de facto cooperation. If one state taxes corporations too heavily, it knows business will move elsewhere. (Those familiar with older debates about "fiscal federalism" within the United States and other nations will recognize the similarity between those issues and the emerging international debates about deeper integration of national economies.) Analogously, differences among nations in regulations, standards, policies, institutions, and even social and cultural preferences create economic incentives for a kind of arbitrage that erodes or eliminates the differences. Such pressures involve not only the conventional arbitrage that exploits price differentials (buying at one point in geographic space or time and selling at another) but also shifts in the location of production facilities and in the residence of factors of production.

In many other cases, however, cross-border spillovers, arbitrage pressures, and diminished effectiveness of national policies can produce unwanted consequences. In cases involving what economists call externalities (external economies and diseconomies), national governments may need to cooperate to promote mutual interests. For example, population growth, continued urbanization, and the more intensive exploitation of natural resources generate external diseconomies not only within but across national boundaries. External economies generated when benefits spill across national jurisdictions probably also increase in importance (for instance, the gains from basic research and from control of communicable diseases).

None of these situations is new, but technological change and the reduction of tariffs and quotas heighten their importance. When one nation produces goods (such as scientific research) or "bads" (such as pollution) that significantly affect other nations, individual governments acting sequentially and noncooperatively cannot deal effectively with the resulting issues. In the absence of explicit cooperation and political leadership, too few collective goods and too many collective bads will be supplied.

Challenges to Political Sovereignty

The pressures from cross-border economic integration sometimes even lead individuals or governments to challenge the core assumptions of national political sovereignty. Such challenges are a third source of tensions about deeper integration.

The existing world system of nation-states assumes that a nation's residents are free to follow their own values and to select their own political arrangements without interference from others. Similarly, property rights are allocated by nation. (The so-called global commons, such as outer space and the deep seabed, are the sole exceptions.) A nation is assumed to have the sovereign right to exploit its property in accordance with its own preferences and policies. Political sovereignty is thus analogous to the concept of consumer sovereignty (the presumption that the individual consumer best knows his or her own interests and should exercise them freely).

In times of war, some nations have had sovereignty wrested from them by force. In earlier eras, a handful of individuals or groups have questioned the premises of political sovereignty. With the profound increases in economic integration in recent decades, however, a larger number of individuals and groups—and occasionally even their national governments—have identified circumstances in which, it is claimed, some universal or international set of values should take precedence over the preferences or policies of particular nations.

Some groups seize on human-rights issues, for example, or what they deem to be egregiously inappropriate political arrangements in other nations. An especially prominent case occurred when citizens in many nations labeled the former apartheid policies of South Africa an affront to universal values and emphasized that the South African government was not legitimately representing the interests of a majority of South Africa's residents. Such views caused many national governments to apply economic sanctions against South Africa. Examples of value conflicts are not restricted to human rights, however. Groups focusing on environmental issues characterize tropical rain forests as the lungs of the world and the genetic repository for numerous species of plants and animals that are the heritage of all mankind. Such views lead Europeans, North Americans, or Japanese to challenge the timber-cutting policies of Brazilians and Indonesians. A recent controversy over tuna fishing with long drift nets that kill porpoises is yet another example. Environmentalists in the United States whose sensibilities were offended by the drowning of porpoises required U.S. boats at some additional expense to amend their fishing practices. The U.S. fishermen, complaining about imported tuna caught with less regard for porpoises, persuaded the U.S. government to ban such tuna imports (both direct imports from the countries in which the tuna is caught and indirect imports shipped via third countries). Mexico and Venezuela were the main countries affected by this ban; a GATT dispute panel sided with Mexico against the United States in the controversy, which further upset the U.S. environmental community.

A common feature of all such examples is the existence, real or alleged, of "psychological externalities" or "political failures." Those holding such views reject untrammeled political sovereignty for nation-states in deference to universal or non-national values. They wish to constrain the exercise of individual nations' sovereignties through international negotiations or, if necessary, by even stronger intervention.

The Management of International Convergence

In areas in which arbitrage pressures and cross-border spillovers are weak and psychological or political externalities are largely absent, national governments may encounter few problems with deeper integration. Diversity across nations may persist quite easily. But at the other extreme, arbitrage and spillovers in some areas may be so strong that they threaten to erode national diversity completely. Or psychological and political sensitivities may be asserted too powerfully to be ignored. Governments will then be confronted with serious tensions, and national policies and behaviors may eventually converge to common, worldwide patterns (for example, subject to internationally agreed norms or minimum standards). Eventual convergence across nations, if it occurs, could happen in a harmful way (national policies and practices being driven to a least common denominator with externalities ignored, in effect a "race to the bottom") or it could occur with mutually beneficial results ("survival of the fittest and the best").

Each study in this series addresses basic questions about the management of international convergence: if, when, and how national governments should intervene to try to influence the consequences of arbitrage pressures, cross-border spillovers, diminished autonomy, and the assertion of psychological or political externalities. A wide variety of responses is conceivable. We identify six, which should be regarded not as distinct categories but as ranges along a continuum.

National autonomy defines a situation at one end of the continuum in which national governments make decentralized decisions with little or no consultation and no explicit cooperation. This response represents political sovereignty at its strongest, undiluted by any international management of convergence.

Mutual recognition, like national autonomy, presumes decentralized decisions by national governments and relies on market competition to guide the process of international convergence. Mutual recognition, however, entails exchanges of information and consultations among governments to constrain the formation of national regulations and policies. As understood in discussions of economic integration within the European Community, moreover, mutual recognition entails an explicit acceptance by each member nation of the regulations, standards, and certification procedures of other members. For example, mutual recognition allows wine or liquor produced in any European Union country to be sold in all twelve member countries even if production standards in member countries differ. Doctors licensed in France are permitted to practice in Germany, and vice versa, even if licensing procedures in the two countries differ.

Governments may agree on rules that restrict their freedom to set policy or that promote gradual convergence in the structure of policy. As international consultations and monitoring of compliance with such rules become more important, this situation can be described as *monitored decentralization*. The Group of Seven finance ministers meetings, supplemented by the IMF's surveillance over exchange rate and macroeconomic policies, illustrate this approach to management.

Coordination goes further than mutual recognition and monitored decentralization in acknowledging convergence pressures. It is also more ambitious in promoting intergovernmental cooperation to deal with them. Coordination involves jointly designed mutual adjustments of national policies. In clear-cut cases of coordination, bargaining occurs and governments agree to behave differently from the ways they would have behaved without the agreement. Examples include the World Health Organization's procedures for controlling communicable diseases and the 1987 Montreal Protocol (to a 1985 framework convention) for the protection of stratospheric ozone by reducing emissions of chlorofluorocarbons.

Explicit harmonization, which requires still higher levels of intergovernmental cooperation, may require agreement on regional standards or world standards. Explicit harmonization typically entails still greater departures from decentralization in decisionmaking and still further strengthening of international institutions. The 1988 agreement among major central banks to set minimum standards for the required capital positions of commercial banks (reached through the Committee on Banking Regulations and Supervisory Practices at the Bank for International Settlements) is an example of partially harmonized regulations.

At the opposite end of the spectrum from national autonomy lies *federalist mutual governance*, which implies continuous bargaining and joint, centralized decisionmaking. To make federalist mutual governance work would require greatly strengthened supranational institutions. This end of the management spectrum, now relevant only as an analytical benchmark, is a possible outcome that can be imagined for the middle or late decades of the twenty-first century, possibly even sooner for regional groupings like the European Union.

Overview of the Brookings Project

Despite their growing importance, the issues of deeper economic integration and its competition with national political sovereignty were largely neglected in the 1980s. In 1992 the Brookings Institution initiated its project on Integrating National Economies to direct attention to these important questions.

In studying this topic, Brookings sought and received the co-operation of some of the world's leading economists, political scientists, foreign-policy specialists, and government officials, representing all regions of the world. Although some functional areas require a special focus on European, Japanese, and North American perspectives, at all junctures the goal was to include, in addition, the perspectives of developing nations and the formerly centrally planned economies.

The first phase of the project commissioned the twenty-one scholarly studies listed at the beginning of the book. One or two lead discussants, typically residents of parts of the world other than the area where the author resides, were asked to comment on each study.

Authors enjoyed substantial freedom to design their individual studies, taking due account of the overall themes and goals of the project. The guidelines for the studies requested that at least some of the analysis be carried out with a non-normative perspective. In effect, authors were asked to develop a "baseline" of what might happen in the absence of changed policies or further international cooperation. For their normative analyses, authors were asked to start with an agnostic posture that did not prejudge the net benefits or costs resulting from integration. The project organizers themselves had no presumption about whether national diversity is better or worse than international convergence or about what the individual studies should conclude regarding the desirability of increased integration. On the contrary, each author was asked to address the trade-offs in his or her issue area between diversity and convergence and to locate the area, currently and prospectively, on the spectrum of international management possibilities running between national autonomy through mutual recognition to coordination and explicit harmonization.

HENRY J. AARON   SUSAN M. COLLINS
RALPH C. BRYANT   ROBERT Z. LAWRENCE

Chapter 1

Introduction

THE most important lesson to be gleaned from recent research in international monetary economics is that the exchange rate is an asset price. Like movements in the Standard and Poor's stock price index, exchange rate fluctuations reflect investors' changing perceptions of prospective capital gains and losses. In the same way that the demand for industrial shares fluctuates with new information, so too does the demand for foreign exchange.

Although this analogy is widely appreciated—not least by investors—in most policy discussions it is set aside. No one argues for stabilizing the Standard and Poor's index, movements in which convey important signals about resource allocation. Yet many policymakers and scholars insist on the need to stabilize the exchange rate, despite the fact that it can be seen as playing the same kind of allocational role.[1] No one argues the need for international cooperation to manage the Standard and Poor's index, although shares are held by investors in many countries. Yet there exists a long history of international conventions to stabilize exchange rates. No one proposes establishing international institutions with responsibility for regulating stock price movements. Yet the International Monetary

1. The analogy between the allocational role of stock prices and exchange rates is explicit in recent theory. See for example Murphy (1989); Gavin (1992). One possible explanation for the different ways in which the two sets of prices are regarded is that changes in equity prices affect mainly the distribution of wealth among different asset holders, whereas changes in the prices of currencies affect the distribution of income between labor and capital and the incidence of unemployment; these last effects are therefore more likely to lead to the formation of the kind of broad-based political coalitions that call for government intervention and management.

1

Fund is only the most recent organization created with the goal of limiting exchange rate fluctuations.

What then could justify the proliferation of schemes to regulate—in the limit to fix—exchange rates between national currencies? One justification is that the exchange rate is the single most important price in the economy.[2] A change in its level can alter the prices in home currency of all the foreign goods against which domestic producers compete.[3] Such a change can induce the wholesale reallocation of resources between sectors producing traded and nontraded goods. Uncontrolled exchange rate fluctuations to which households and firms find it difficult to adjust can therefore impose significant costs. Those who subscribe to this reasoning argue for an international monetary system that minimizes superfluous exchange rate fluctuations and ensures the orderliness of necessary changes.[4]

These arguments are most compelling to those who are skeptical about the efficiency of the foreign exchange market. They indict exchange rates for excessive volatility, faulting them for fluctuating more widely than is justified by fundamentals.[5] Currency traders, they suggest, are susceptible to fads and fashions, oscillating between excessive optimism and undue pessimism.[6] If there exist costs of deviations of exchange rates from their long-term equilibrium levels, then there may be grounds for policy intervention to prevent unwarranted fluctuations.

Arguments such as these provide a rationale for government intervention in the foreign exchange market. But why should they encourage the establishment of rules and institutions to facilitate the joint management of exchange rates by a collectivity of countries? The obvious answer is that the exchange rate, as the relative price of two currencies, is affected by the policies of both of the issuing governments. Officials anxious to achieve reelection or reappointment will

2. See Kenen (1992).

3. The extent of the relative price change induced by a movement in the exchange rate depends on the structure of the relevant markets. These questions are the subject of the literature on exchange rate pass-through. See, for example, Mann (1986); Dornbusch (1987).

4. See, for example, McKinnon (1990).

5. See Woo (1985); West (1987). These two studies of the foreign exchange market reach this conclusion by building on Shiller's (1989) influential work on the excess volatility of stock prices but applying the methodology to the foreign exchange market.

6. The implications of these possibilities are explored by Frankel and Froot (1988); Froot and Thaler (1990).

concentrate on the impact of policies on their constituencies to the neglect of foreign repercussions. They may fail to take into account the implications of their policies for the foreign exchange market and hence for their foreign counterparts. International cooperation in managing exchange rates may be a way of achieving the coordination of national economic policies from which all countries benefit.[7] To prevent governments from reneging on their pledge to cooperate, it may be necessary to establish institutions for pooling information, monitoring compliance, and sanctioning defectors.

The Debate over International Monetary Reform

The debate over international monetary reform is typically framed as a contest between fixed and flexible rates. Milton Friedman, in his 1953 paper "The Case for Flexible Exchange Rates," argued that the rationale for regulating the price of foreign exchange is no better than that for pegging the price of carrots or potatoes. Kindleberger, McKinnon, and others have been equally eloquent in articulating the case for fixed rates.[8] A panoply of theoretical models has been deployed to analyze the conditions under which one or the other of these arrangements delivers desirable results.

Given the terms of the debate, it is ironic that international systems of durably pegged and freely floating exchange rates are almost never observed. Certainly particular countries have maintained one or the other arrangement for limited periods. France in the first half of the 1920s allowed the franc to float freely. The United States left the dollar to float free of intervention in the first half of the 1980s.[9] Italy floated the lira following its exit from the European Monetary System (EMS) in 1992. Luxembourg since World War II has fixed its franc to that of Belgium. Argentina pegs to the U.S. dollar, Austria and Estonia to the German mark. But these are policies adopted unilaterally by individual countries. They do not constitute *international* monetary systems.

7. This is the insight of the literature on international economic policy coordination; see Bryant (forthcoming) for a survey. Canzoneri and Gray (1985) were the first to analyze the conditions under which an exchange rate stabilization agreement could be an effective means of ensuring the optimal coordination of national macroeconomic policies.

8. See Friedman (1953); Kindleberger (1981); McKinnon (1990).

9. The very few exceptions to this policy are enumerated by Frankel (1994).

Virtually all international monetary regimes with which the world has had experience lie in the no-man's-land between fixed and freely floating rates. Governments intervene to stabilize the foreign exchange value of their currencies, but not continuously. They resist some exchange rate fluctuations, but not others. In effect, every international monetary system has been a hybrid of fixed and floating rates.

It is possible to go beyond this characterization to describe more precisely the kind of international monetary arrangements that governments generally prefer. These have tended to be contingent rules defined in terms of exchange rate targets. Policymakers commit to holding the exchange rate within a band against a reference currency under all but exceptional circumstances. These compromise arrangements sail under the banners of "pegged but adjustable exchange rates," "crawling pegs," and "exchange rate target zones."

Such arrangements are a compromise between otherwise incompatible objectives. They seek to reconcile the desire for autonomy for national stabilization policies with the goal of restraining inflation and promoting international economic integration. In general, it will not be optimal to commit to a system of permanently fixed exchange rates that constrains national policy under all circumstances. Nor will it be optimal to choose a system of freely floating rates under which policymakers are unprotected from pressures to inflate and free to disregard the impact of domestic policies on foreign countries. In principle, a contingent exchange rate target combines the advantages of fixed and floating rates by providing stability, predictability, and anti-inflationary credibility in normal times, along with the flexibility under exceptional circumstances to adjust policies that are otherwise constrained by the exchange rate target.

The Argument

The argument of this book is that contingent policy rules designed to hit explicit exchange rate targets will no longer be viable in the twenty-first century.[10] It will not be possible to maintain arrange-

10. Like virtually all arguments in economics, this one is not without precedent. The clearest prior statement I have been able to find is Cooper (1984). A similar argument was advanced by Crockett (1994) in a paper circulated and published after the first draft of this book was completed. Kenen (1988) argued that growing international capital mobility will

ments under which governments commit to preventing exchange rate movements from exceeding explicit limits under all but specific circumstances. This will rule out the maintenance for extended periods of pegged but adjustable exchange rates, crawling pegs, and other regimes in which governments pre-announce limits on exchange rate fluctuations and intervene to prevent their violation under all but exceptional circumstances. Calls for international monetary reform to reestablish a system of pegged but adjustable rates will therefore prove futile.[11] Similar objections can be advanced to the Williamson target zone proposal.[12] The implication is that countries that have traditionally pegged their currencies will be forced to choose between floating exchange rates on the one hand and monetary unification on the other.[13]

This argument is derived from a model in which the viability of international monetary arrangements hinges on three conditions: the ability to effect relative price adjustments, compatibility with the pursuit of robust monetary policies, and a capacity to contain market pressures. The viability of international monetary systems past, from the classical gold standard to the Bretton Woods System and the EMS, can be understood in terms of their success in satisfying these three conditions. In the future, in contrast, changes in technology, market structure, and politics will undermine the viability of such arrangements. The institutionalized structure of labor markets will restrict the fluidity with which prices and wages adjust to shocks, heightening the importance of exchange rate changes for effecting adjustment. The increasingly politicized environment in which monetary policy is made will erode the credibility of governments' commitment to the pursuit of robust mone-

---

rule out the maintenance of pegged but adjustable rates, forcing countries to choose between fixed and floating currencies. In arguing that fixed rates between distinct national currencies are no longer viable and that the choice is between floating and monetary unification, I am in a sense merely taking his argument forward another step.

11. Such calls have included those by Krugman (1990); McKinnon (1990).

12. See Williamson (1985); Williamson and Miller (1987). The multifaceted nature of this proposal renders its compatibility with the prerequisites for a viable international monetary system contingent on the particular variant of the proposal under consideration. For this reason and because the target zone proposal has been the subject of so much recent attention, I address the issues it raises in chapter 5.

13. As I go to considerable lengths to make clear, floating does not mean that exchange rates cannot be managed—in other words, that policy cannot be adjusted in response to currency fluctuations. What it does mean, as explained in chapter 5, is that policy rules framed in terms of explicit, binding exchange rate targets will not be viable.

tary rules. Above all, changes in technology will work to increase international capital mobility, limiting the capacity of governments to contain market pressures at an acceptable political cost. Together these changes will undermine the viability of the monetary rules under which governments commit to preventing exchange rates from breeching certain limits under all but exceptional circumstances, forcing policy-makers to choose between floating and monetary unification.

To be clear, the argument is not that *free* floating and monetary union are the only viable international monetary options for the twenty-first century. Countries will still be able to adjust their money supplies in response to exchange rate fluctuations. What they will not be able to do is to peg their exchange rates successfully for significant periods of time. Regimes of pegged but adjustable rates like the Bretton Woods System and the EMS of the 1980s, in which govern-ments attempted to hold their exchange rates within narrow bands, except under exceptional circumstances, will no longer be viable. Crawling pegs, which differ only in that governments allow the band to shift continuously in response to ongoing inflation differentials, will be similarly problematic, as will many proposals for exchange rate target zones.

These pressures are already evident in recent trends in exchange rate arrangements. Between 1982 and 1993 the share of countries with independently floating exchange rates rose from 5 to 32 percent. Meanwhile, one set of countries with a particularly strong attraction to pegging, the twelve members of the European Community (now the European Union), embarked on a concerted effort to establish a monetary union by the end of the decade. However, it was forced in 1993 to abandon its attempt to peg intra-European exchange rates within narrow bands, a fact that can be taken as further support of the premise of this book. A number of countries attempting to hold their exchange rates unilaterally within narrow bands have been forced to widen the band significantly (as in Chile) or to abandon it altogether (as in Finland and Sweden).[14] Already the middle ground of pegged but adjustable rates and narrow target zones is being hollowed out.

In which direction countries should move is not obvious. The choice between floating and monetary unification depends on a host

---

14. Where target zones have been more successfully maintained (as in Israel), this reflects the maintenance of capital controls, which reinforce the capacity to contain market pressures.

of cross-cutting factors. A rational decision depends not just on economic considerations but also on political considerations. Given its implications for a wide range of economic and political objectives, this choice will emerge as perhaps the single most important economic policy decision for governments and their constituencies at the dawn of the twenty-first century.

Organization of This Book

The remainder of this book, which elaborates on these points, is organized as follows. Chapter 2 describes the menu of international monetary arrangements from which policymakers have traditionally selected. It emphasizes the advantages of a system of internationally agreed-upon exchange rates as compared to a collection of unilateral national arrangements. Chapter 3 introduces the three conditions that any adequate international monetary system must satisfy: the ability to effect relative price adjustments, compatibility with the pursuit of robust monetary rules, and a capacity to contain market pressures. Chapter 4 illustrates the indispensability of these requirements with a look back at the history of the international monetary system, showing how the ability of international monetary regimes past to meet these conditions explains their viability and how their subsequent failure to meet one or more of them explains their eventual demise.

Chapter 5 is the core of the book: it explains why many of the entrees on the traditional menu are no longer palatable. It analyzes which of the preconditions for a viable international monetary system will be impossible to satisfy in the twenty-first century by most of the arrangements that aspiring reformers continue to contemplate. It shows that international capital mobility will limit the capacity to contain market pressures at an acceptable cost. It argues that changes in the political environment will irrevocably compromise the credibility of governments' commitment to the pursuit of robust monetary rules. These changes, it concludes, will rule out contingent policy rules designed to hit explicit exchange rate targets.

Chapter 6 enumerates the considerations that should enter into the selection of an option from the limited list of viable international monetary arrangements for the twenty-first century. The next two chapters use this list to explain recent tendencies toward pegged exchange rates and perhaps even monetary unification in some parts of the world but increased reliance on floating rates in others. Given that the most dramatic international monetary initiatives are those currently underway in Western Europe, a separate chapter (the seventh) is devoted to that region's experience. The recent trials and tribulations of the EMS illustrate the increasing difficulty of operating systems of pegged but adjustable exchange rates and highlight the prominence of political considerations in the choice between free floating and monetary unification. I conclude that, despite the recent crisis in the EMS and growing doubts about the adequacy of the Maastricht Treaty, prospects for monetary union remain brighter in Europe than in other parts of the world.

Comparisons with Asia, Africa, the former Soviet Union, and the Western Hemisphere are considered in chapter 8. I conjecture that many of these regions, like Europe before them, will seek to move away from floating exchange rates. Outside Europe, however, the political and economic preconditions for monetary union are less well developed. Countries in these regions are therefore likely to experiment with unilateral pegs, unilateral target zones, and EMS-like arrangements. If the premise of this book is correct, such arrangements will be at best temporarily successful, representing for some a way station on the road to monetary union and for others a brief respite from floating.

It is conceivable that, with the passage of time, regional monetary unions will emerge not just in Europe but also in the Western Hemisphere and even possibly in East Asia. Some commentators suggest that these regional arrangements might in turn evolve into a single world currency by the middle of the twenty-first century.[15] Insofar as ongoing economic integration renders floating exchange rates less desirable, there will be pressure in this direction. But however impeccable the economic logic for a single world currency, the political preconditions are unlikely to be in place. Establishing even a regionally limited monetary union poses formidable problems of governance and accountability, as Europe continues to learn. The assumption that these can be surmounted on a global scale will remain heroic for years to come.

15. See Cooper (1990); Bergsten (1993).

Chapter 2

Policy Options

*T*HE problem of selecting from the menu of options for international monetary reform will be familiar to patrons of Chinese restaurants. Each diner may prefer to place his or her own order. The table will ultimately receive an interesting array of platters, but several individually ordered and consumed dishes will not constitute a banquet. Similarly each country may choose to float its exchange rate, to peg, or to adopt a target zone. But the sum of these decentralized exchange rate policy decisions will not necessarily constitute a coherent international monetary system.

The other approach is for the diners to coordinate: to agree on an order of which all will partake. This should enable them to consume a meal with a wider assortment of desirable features. Indivisibilities may permit the kitchen to produce dishes like Peking duck that could not be economically served to a single patron. In the international monetary context, a group of countries may agree to a system of pegged but adjustable exchange rates with international credit lines, to a managed float with reciprocal intervention obligations, or to a monetary union; none of these options is available to a government acting alone.

The viability of such arrangements is contingent upon the participation of countries with compatible tastes, in the same way that the attractions of the banquet depend on the participation of a party of like-minded diners. Coordinating an order, moreover, poses logistical problems. How can one be sure that the tastes of all diners will be accommodated? How can one be assured that all the essential food groups will be represented? How can special dietary needs be met?

9

Whatever the strategy chosen for ordering dinner, the process necessarily starts by considering the individual dishes on offer. This chapter proceeds in like fashion, first enumerating the options for exchange rate policy that may be pursued by countries unilaterally and only then considering the possibilities for collectively establishing an international monetary system. It is designed to highlight the contrast between these two approaches to developing an international monetary order.[1] It emphasizes the advantages of a system of internationally agreed-upon exchange rates as opposed to a collection of unilateral national arrangements.

Ordering à la Carte

This section considers the policy choices available to countries acting unilaterally.

Freely Floating Exchange Rates

The simplest option for exchange rate policy is freely floating rates. However desirable economically or viable politically it may ultimately prove, this arrangement is a limiting case and therefore a benchmark against which other options are gauged.

The literature on the merits and limitations of floating rates is too vast to be usefully surveyed here. Suffice it to say that policymakers have shown by revealed preference an aversion to relying for extended periods on freely floating rates. As noted in chapter 1, interludes of free floating are not hard to identify. But all such episodes are limited in duration—the strategy tends to be superseded by other arrangements for managing exchange rates.

Three characteristics of freely floating exchange rates are conducive to this propensity. First, nominal exchange rate fluctuations can lead to large changes in relative national price levels. (Figure 2-1 shows a case in point: the U.S. dollar in the 1980s.) Persistent real exchange rate movements, which will be costly for at least some

---

1. Logically, the analysis might begin with a more fundamental question, namely whether it is worthwhile to go to the restaurant at all. In other words, if a country starts with a clean slate it might first decide whether it even wants to have a money of its own. For most countries the question does not pose itself in this way, however, since they already possess national monies.

Figure 2-1. *Nominal and Real Effective Exchange Rates,*
U.S. Dollar, 1973–90

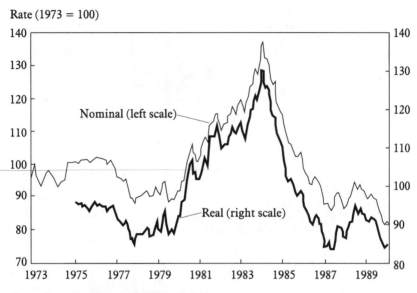

Source: *International Financial Statistics*, various issues.

economic interest groups, can result.[2] Second, even if purchasing
power parity is quickly restored (persistent misalignments are not a
problem), floating rates tend to be associated with increased relative
price variability, making it hard to distinguish temporary from permanent changes in relative prices and to allocate resources efficiently.[3]
Figure 2-2 illustrates this point for three major exchange rates under
the Bretton Woods system and the post–Bretton Woods float. And
third, allowing the exchange rate to float without restriction may
remove a nominal anchor useful for stabilizing price expectations and
disciplining macroeconomic policymakers.

2. Williamson (1985) provides a catalogue of the costs of real exchange rate misalignment; these include capricious changes in households' purchasing power, costs of adjustment for firms, induced unemployment, misdirected investment, added inflation, and
increased protectionist pressure.

3. Two studies that make this point are Rogoff (1985b) and Artis and Taylor (1988). It
is conceivable, according to Stockman (1987a), that the increase in real exchange rate
volatility in periods of floating reflects an increased prevalence of real shocks that destabilize
both real and nominal rates. Krugman (1990) rebuts this view. Tamim Bayoumi and I
(1994c) have attempted to measure such disturbances for the industrial economies, finding
little evidence of a significant increase in the magnitude of real disturbances between
Bretton Woods and the post–Bretton Woods float.

Figure 2-2. *Monthly Percent Change in Real Exchange Rates, 1960–90*

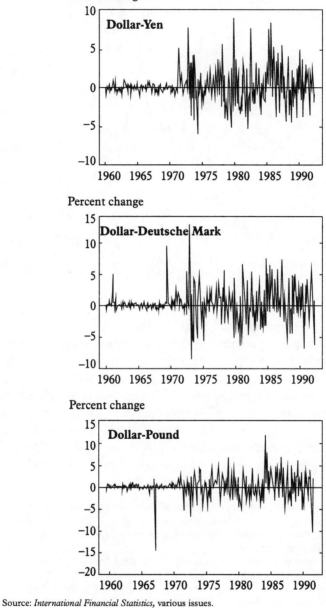

Source: *International Financial Statistics*, various issues.

For all these reasons, freely floating exchange rates are very much the exception to the rule.

Managed Floating

Under managed floating, exchange rates are allowed to fluctuate but are subject to intervention. Beyond this statement it is difficult to generalize about managed floating exchange rates as a class.

One distinction worth emphasizing is that between managed floating in general (when exchange rate management takes place but is not framed in terms of an exchange rate target) and exchange rate targeting in particular. One-third to one-half of International Monetary Fund (IMF) member countries follow some form of managed floating (table 2-1 as of September 1993). The majority of these countries peg to a single currency, the SDR (Special Drawing Rights), or a currency basket, or limit the flexibility of their currencies vis-à-vis a single currency or a composite; all these countries, in other words, frame policy in terms of an exchange rate target. A somewhat smaller number of countries adjust their rates according to a set of (non-exchange-rate) indicators (table 2-2).

Furthermore, the share of countries whose exchange rates float, under various degrees of management, has risen from less than one-fifth of all IMF members in 1975 to one-third in 1982 and fully half in 1993. This is no coincidence, as I argue in chapter 5.

A common approach to managed floating is leaning against the wind. When the exchange rate weakens, the central bank or government intervenes to support it. When it strengthens, the bank or government intervenes to limit its appreciation. However, the timing and quantity of intervention are not guided by an explicit exchange rate target.[4]

A common rationale for this policy is that many exchange rate fluctuations are temporary and as such confer unnecessary costs. If the nominal rate appreciates currently but will depreciate subsequently, leaning against the wind can reduce the costs associated with that temporary fluctuation. It is not clear, however, why currency

4. See Tosini (1977). An example of this policy is Canada in the 1950s, then the only industrial country with a floating rate. In 100 of 123 months from October 1950 through December 1960, the Canadian Exchange Fund Account acquired reserves when the currency was strengthening and expended reserves when it was weakening. See Yeager (1966, p. 426).

Table 2-1. *Exchange Rate Arrangements of International Monetary Fund Member Countries as of December 31, 1993*[a]

Currency pegged to:					Flexibility limited in terms of a single currency or group of currencies		More flexible		
U.S. dollar	French franc	Other currency	SDR	Other composite [b]	Single currency [c]	Cooperative arrangements [d]	Adjusted according to a set of indicators	Other managed floating	Independently floating
Angola	Benin	Azerbaijan (Russian ruble)	Libya	Algeria	Bahrain	Belgium	Chile	Belarus	Afghanistan	Tanzania
Antigua and Barbuda	Burkina Faso	Bhutan (Indian rupee)	Myanmar	Austria	Qatar	Denmark	Colombia	Cambodia	Albania	Trinidad and Tobago
Argentina	Cameroon	Estonia (deutsche mark)	Rwanda	Bangladesh	Saudi Arabia	France	Madagascar	China, People's Republic of	Armenia	Uganda
Bahamas, The	Central African Republic	Kiribati (Australian dollar)	Seychelles	Botswana	United Arab Emirates	Germany	Nicaragua	Ecuador	Australia	Ukraine
Barbados	Chad	Lesotho (South African rand)		Burundi		Ireland		Egypt	Bolivia	United Kingdom
Belize	Comoros	Namibia (South African rand)		Cape Verde		Luxembourg		Greece	Brazil	United States
Djibouti	Congo	San Marino (Italian lira)		Cyprus		Netherlands		Guinea	Bulgaria	Zaire
Dominica	Côte d'Ivoire	Swaziland (South African rand)		Czech Republic		Portugal		Guinea-Bissau	Canada	Zambia
Grenada	Equatorial Guinea			Fiji		Spain		Indonesia	Costa Rica	
Iraq	Gabon			Hungary				Israel	Croatia	
Liberia	Mali			Iceland				Korea	Dominican Republic	
Marshall Islands	Niger			Jordan				Lao P.D. Republic	El Salvador	
Micronesia, Federated States of	Senegal			Kuwait				Malaysia	Ethiopia	
Oman	Togo			Malawi				Maldives	Finland	
Panama				Malta				Mexico	Gambia, The	
St. Kitts and Nevis				Mauritania				Pakistan	Georgia	
St. Lucia				Mauritius				Poland	Ghana	
St. Vincent and Grenadines				Morocco				Sao Tome and Principe	Guatemala	
Suriname				Nepal				Singapore	Guyana	
				Papua New Guinea				Slovenia	Haiti	
				Solomon Islands					Honduras	
				Thailand					India	
				Tonga					Iran	

Syria	Vanuatu	Somalia	Italy
Yemen,	Western	Sri Lanka	Jamaica
Republic of	Samoa	Sudan	Japan
	Zimbabwe	Tunisia	Kazakhstan
		Turkey	Kenya
		Turkmenistan	Kyrgyz Republic
		Uruguay	Latvia
		Venezuela	Lebanon
		Vietnam	Lithuania
			Macedonia
			Moldova
			Mongolia
			Mozambique
			New Zealand
			Nigeria
			Norway
			Paraguay
			Peru
			Philippines
			Romania
			Russia
			Sierra Leone
			South Africa
			Sweden
			Switzerland

Source: *International Financial Statistics*, May 1994, p. 8.
a. For members with dual or multiple exchange markets, the arrangement shown is that in the major market. Includes exchange arrangements under which the exchange rate is adjusted at relatively frequent intervals, on the basis of indicators determined by the respective member countries.
b. Comprises currencies that are pegged to various "baskets" of currencies of the members' own choice, as distinct from the SDR basket.
c. Exchange rates of all currencies have shown limited flexibility in terms of the U.S. dollar.
d. Refers to the cooperative arrangement maintained under the European Monetary System.

Table 2-2. *Exchange Rate Arrangements, 1987–93*

End of period

Classification status[a]	1987	1988	1989	1990	1991 QII	1991 QIII	1991 QIV	1992 QI	1992 QII	1992 QIII	1992 QIV	1993 QI	1993 QII	1993 QIII	1993 QIV
Currency pegged to:															
U.S. dollar	38	36	32	25	26	25	24	23	24	26	24	23	20	20	21
French franc	14	14	14	14	14	14	14	14	14	14	14	14	14	14	14
Russian ruble	…	…	…	…	…	…	…	…	…	5	6	7	7	5	…[b]
Other currency	5	5	5	5	5	5	4	4	5	6	6	6	6	7	8
SDR	8	7	7	6	6	6	6	6	5	5	5	4	4	4	4
Other currency composite	27	31	35	35	35	34	33	32	32	31	29	27	27	26	26
Flexibility limited vis-à-vis a single currency	4	4	4	4	4	4	4	4	4	4	4	4	4	4	4
Cooperative arrangements	8	8	9	9	10	10	10	10	10	11	9	9	9	9	9
Adjusted according to a set of indicators	5	5	5	3	5	5	5	5	4	4	3	4	4	4	4
Managed floating	23	22	21	23	22	23	27	25	23	22	23	21	27	27	29
Independently floating	18	17	20	25	28	29	29	33	36	41	44	48	49	52	56
Total[c]	151	151	152	154	155	155	156	156	158	167	167	167	171	172	175

Source: *International Financial Statistics*, May 1994, p. 8.

a. For members with dual or multiple exchange markets, the arrangement shown is that in the major market. Includes exchange arrangements under which the exchange rate is adjusted at relatively frequent intervals, on the basis of indicators determined by the respective member countries.

b. One country, Azerbaijan, continues to peg its currency, the manat, against the Russian ruble and has been added to the group of countries whose currencies are classified under "Currency pegged to: Other currency."

c. Excluding the following three countries, which as of the end of December 1993 have not yet formally notified the IMF of their exchange rate arrangements: Slovak Republic, Tajikistan, and Uzbekistan.

traders, cognizant of this pattern, would not buy currencies that have weakened (and sell those that have strengthened) in anticipation of future capital gains, thereby damping temporary fluctuations and obviating the need for the authorities to lean against the wind.[5] Thus, this argument for intervention fundamentally rests on the inefficiency of the market.[6]

All this glosses over the question of which instruments are used for intervention, an issue whose relevance extends beyond managed floating. The debate revolves around the question of whether it is possible for policymakers to alter the exchange rate without changing money supplies.[7] If domestic and foreign interest-bearing assets are perfect substitutes, capital is mobile, and sterilized intervention (equivalently, a swap of domestic and foreign bonds) conveys no information about future policies, then the only way in which the authorities can affect the exchange rate is by altering money supplies. This is not to say that exchange rate management is impossible, only that other objectives of monetary policy have to be sacrificed in order to attain an exchange rate target. In contrast, if domestic and foreign assets are imperfect substitutes, then an open market operation (say, a sale of foreign bonds for domestic currency) that is sterilized (through a purchase of domestic bonds for domestic currency) can alter the exchange rate

5. This observation was the basis for Friedman's (1953) argument that exchange rate fluctuations should be smoothed by stabilizing speculation. A related argument is that agents can protect themselves against any associated costs through recourse to the forward market.

6. There is by now a vast literature on the inefficiency of foreign exchange markets; see, for example, Hansen and Hodrick (1980). Much of it focuses on the inefficiency of the forward market—that is, on the failure of the forward discount to predict accurately depreciation over the contract period. An alternative view is that, absent intervention, most of the shocks driving exchange rate changes are permanent. Recent statistical work suggesting that exchange rates follow a random walk is consistent with this conclusion. If the authorities do not alter the policy variables under their control in ways that offset the impact on the exchange rate of those shocks, there is no reason for investors to engage in stabilizing speculation. If, in contrast, the authorities are expected to lean against the wind, market participants will learn to anticipate their actions. They will buy the currency in advance of official purchases, minimizing the intervention needed to achieve any degree of exchange rate stabilization. This is a theme of the literature on exchange rate target zones; I return to it in that context.

7. See, for example, Rogoff (1984); Obstfeld (1988). This discussion, focusing on monetary policy, defers until later a consideration of the role of fiscal policy in influencing the exchange rate. The relevant point in the present context is that, compared to monetary instruments, fiscal policy is hard to fine tune in response to exchange rate fluctuations. This may be critically important when pegged rates come under attack, as explained in chapter 5.

(one of the relative prices in financial markets that equates asset supplies with stock demands) without requiring a change in money supplies.

The evidence suggests that time-varying risk premiums, which must be present if domestic and foreign assets are to be imperfect substitutes, are small and bear no stable relationship to the asset stocks the authorities are capable of influencing. This implies that the scope for sterilized intervention to manage the exchange rate is limited.

If sterilized intervention signals a shift in future monetary policies, it can affect the exchange rate now without requiring a shift in monetary policy until later.[8] The evidence generally points to the existence of a statistically significant signaling effect, which is consistent with recent studies, by Dominguez and Frankel among others, that even sterilized intervention can influence the exchange rate.[9] For signaling to matter, however, it must be backed up eventually by the anticipated changes in money supply. This requires that policy changes be predictable, which brings us to the case of exchange rate target zones.

Target Zones

An exchange rate band or target zone attempts to restrict the rate to a particular interval. Within the band the exchange rate is allowed to float, freely or subject to management, but when the edge of the band is reached, further movement is blocked by concerted intervention. A target zone thus combines elements of pegged and floating exchange rates.

A target zone can be implicit or explicit. For it to be effective, however, the authorities' commitment to defending the exchange rate when it reaches the edge of the band must be credible. If the authorities commit to defending the rate when it reaches the edge of the band, they will enjoy a "target zone honeymoon." Investors will begin buying the currency as it approaches the bottom of the band, since they anticipate that the authorities are committed to buying it, thereby preventing capital losses and making available a one-way bet when

8. The signaling effect was first described by Mussa (1981). Edison (1993) surveys the subsequent literature. The statement in the text applies, strictly speaking, to monetary models of the exchange rate. In other models, signaling may pertain to a future change in other policies as well.

9. See Kaminsky and Lewis (1993); Lewis (1993); Dominguez and Frankel (1993).

the edge of the band is reached. They will begin selling the currency as it approaches the top of the band, since they expect the authorities to sell it when the limit of the band is reached. Their actions reduce, for any set of fundamentals, the probability that the edge of the band will actually be reached. Over a given range of realizations of the fundamentals, this "bias in the band" will stabilize the exchange rate without any intervention.[10]

The attraction of target zones is that they promise to reconcile exchange rate stability with domestic policy autonomy. The rate is allowed to fluctuate only within the band, limiting volatility. But even this limited flexibility provides some autonomy for monetary policy. If the authorities expand the money supply, driving the exchange rate to the bottom of its band, the knowledge that the currency can only appreciate subsequently will render investors willing to hold it at reduced interest rates. Hence monetary policy can be used to affect interest rates—and the macroeconomic aggregates that interest rates influence—even while holding the exchange rate within the band. Domestic policy autonomy is limited: the reduction in interest rates can only be temporary, since it will disappear once the exchange rate recovers to the center of the band.[11] More important, the idea that limited monetary autonomy and exchange rate stability can be reconciled is premised on the notion that the authorities' commitment to defense of the zone is credible, an assumption that cannot be taken for granted.

Much recent attention to target zones emanates from their advocacy by Williamson and Williamson and Miller. These analyses have led to the rediscovery of the fact that all pegged exchange rate systems resemble target zones.[12] Short of monetary unification, exchange rates are never rigidly fixed in practice. Pegging the exchange rate

10. Evidence of the particular S-shaped relationship between the exchange rate and the fundamentals predicted by the early target zone literature, viz. Krugman (1991), is mixed. See Flood, Rose, and Mathieson (1990). Lewis (1990) shows how more realistic intervention rules featuring intramarginal interventions alter the statistical implications of the model.

11. Put another way, a loose monetary policy now which causes the exchange rate to depreciate must be followed by a tight monetary policy later to return it to the middle of the band. These points are modeled by Svensson (1992). Note their relationship to the literature on the signaling effect of sterilized intervention discussed in the preceding subsection.

12. See Williamson (1985); Williamson and Miller (1987). On the resemblance between pegged systems and target zones, see, for example, Giovannini (1989).

means using policy to prevent it from fluctuating beyond prescribed limits—that is, maintaining a narrow band.

Chile, Finland, Israel, Norway, and Sweden have all adopted unilateral target zones. It is worth considering one of these arrangements, Sweden's, in some detail.[13] For much of the 1980s, Sweden's central bank, the Riksbank, pegged the exchange rate to a trade-weighted currency basket.[14] In May 1991, it shifted to an ECU peg. The target value for the exchange rate was specified but the bands around the index were not revealed. Later the Riksbank disclosed that it had been working with a band of plus or minus 2.25 percent. In mid-1985 the band was narrowed to 1.5 percent and openly announced.

From this announcement until November 1992, when it fell prey to the crisis in the European Monetary System (EMS), the krona was continually within its band. The three-month-ahead forward rate, a simple measure of the credibility of the exchange rate, moved outside the band only in mid-1985, when the authorities responded by narrowing their target zone, and toward the end of August 1992 with the mounting crisis. Between September and November 1992, a massive speculative attack was launched against Sweden's target zone. The Riksbank was forced to raise its marginal lending rate to as much as 500 percent in a last-ditch, ultimately unsuccessful effort to hold the krona within its band.

As this experience suggests, the question for proponents of target zones is what lends them credibility. If the band is wide and the authorities do not have occasion to demonstrate their commitment to the exchange rate's defense, why should currency traders believe them when they insist that there exists a point at which they are committed to intervene? Indeed if the markets believe the authorities are inclined to realign (to shift the band when its edge is reached), the target zone honeymoon may be replaced by a target zone divorce, in which the volatility of the exchange rate is amplified as the edge of the band is approached.[15]

13. Many of the details in the paragraphs that follow are from Horngren and Lindberg (1993).

14. Initially the Riksbank had planned to introduce a unilateral deutsche mark peg, but there was confusion about whether this would be acceptable to Germany without the prior approval of the Bundesbank.

15. For theoretical and empirical analyses of this possibility see Bertola and Caballero (1990); Bertola and Svensson (1993).

In theoretical treatments it is assumed that the authorities incur a lump sum cost when violating their commitment to hold the exchange rate within the zone.[16] The market's knowledge that this cost exists lends credibility to their commitment, since it will not be optimal to incur that cost, except under the most unusual circumstances. Indeed, the authorities may seek to influence the size of that cost, since increasing it may enhance their credibility, albeit at the expense of policy flexibility.[17]

This approach is incomplete for two reasons. First, it is not clear what the fixed cost is, how it is determined, and how its magnitude can be influenced. Second, the approach ignores problems of incomplete information and moral hazard that complicate any attempt to exploit trade-offs between credibility and flexibility.[18]

Pegged Exchange Rates

A narrow target zone with periodic realignments bears a strong resemblance to a pegged but adjustable rate. Historical examples abound of this kind of exchange rate arrangement. Under the pre–World War I gold standard, countries pegged their currencies to a given quantity of gold and thereby to one another. They did so again from the mid-1920s until the early 1930s. As of December 1993, twenty-one countries pegged their currencies to the U.S. dollar, fourteen (mainly former French West African colonies) to the franc, one former Soviet republic to the Russian ruble, and seven to other currencies. Four nations pegged to the SDR and twenty-six maintained other basket pegs. There has been a significant decline in recent years in the share of countries pegging their currencies: between 1982 and 1993 the share pegging to a single currency dropped from 40 to 25 percent, while the share maintaining a basket peg dropped from 25 to 17 percent. (Here basket pegs include SDR pegs.)

In line with the target zone analogy, exchange rate pegs typically entail a margin within which the rate is allowed to fluctuate and circumstances under which the peg may be altered or abandoned. All

16. See Flood and Isard (1989).

17. See Cukierman, Kiguel, and Leiderman (1993). The larger the fixed cost, the less scope for the authorities to respond flexibly to exceptional shocks but the greater their credibility.

18. These problems are the subject of chapter 3.

so-called "fixed-rate commitments" entail fluctuation bands and contingencies under which the rate may be unfixed. Gold standard
parities, for example, were surrounded by bands of approximately
plus or minus 0.5 percent within which the exchange rate could
fluctuate without occasioning either corrective gold flows or central
bank intervention.[19] Gold standard pegs could be and were changed.
Prior to 1913 most such changes were temporary: countries experiencing financial difficulties suspended gold convertibility temporarily,
allowing their exchange rates to depreciate for a time but restoring
them to their previous level once normalcy returned. After World War
I permanent changes were more common.[20]

The same point applies to crawling pegs, under which the authorities preannounce not a level for the exchange rate but a path.[21] They
announce their intention of allowing the exchange rate to depreciate
against a foreign currency or basket by a certain percent a month.
Even though domestic inflation persistently exceeds foreign inflation,
a crawling peg may deliver many of the benefits of a stable exchange
rate. The question for advocates of a crawling peg, once again, is what
lends credibility to the authorities' commitment to the preannounced
rate of crawl.

This is a controversial issue in countries prone to inflation, where
crawling pegs and fixed rates have been used in stabilization programs. Though the usefulness of an exchange rate peg as a nominal
anchor in the disinflation process is contested, most economists
would reject the extreme view that the exchange rate is irrelevant for
disinflation and stabilization. Most would also reject the heterodox
position that the monetary and fiscal sources of the inflation are mere
by-products of exchange rate instability, so that it is both necessary
and sufficient in order for stabilization that the government peg the
exchange rate. The middle ground is that pegging the exchange rate

19. The edges of these bands were the so-called "gold points." Bloomfield (1959)
remains the definitive reference on this subject.

20. Counterexamples to both generalizations can be found. For example, various Latin
American countries permanently abandoned exchange rate pegs prior to 1913; see Ford
(1962); Fishlow (1989). Britain, in a famous episode, restored its previously abandoned
exchange rate peg in 1925. For a recent analysis emphasizing these aspects of gold standard
pegs, see Bordo and Kydland (1992). I return to the historical evidence on these issues in
chapter 4.

21. Another indication of the close parallels between narrow bands and pegged rates is
that some target zone arrangements (in Chile and Israel, for example) have allowed the
central parity of the band to crawl downward at a preannounced rate.

can usefully buttress the requisite monetary and fiscal measures.[22] By slowing inflation temporarily, it can reveal the share of the budget deficit that is structural and the share that is inflation-induced, clarifying the steps the government must take to put its financial house in order. It can provide a focal point for price and wage setters, solving the coordination problems raised by stabilization.[23]

If pegging reveals that the government has not put its financial house in order, wage and price inflation will not be checked. The exchange rate will become overvalued, and intervention in its support will provoke a steady loss of international reserves. The authorities' commitment to maintaining the peg, whether crawling or fixed, will not be regarded as credible. Anticipating the exhaustion of the country's reserves, speculators will run on the central bank, forcing abandonment of the peg.[24]

Complete Meals (Systemic Options)

The preceding options are for countries going it alone. The alternative is to design exchange rate arrangements at the international level. A message of this section is that a system of internationally agreed-upon exchange rates has advantages over a set of unilateral national arrangements. Those advantages must be weighed against the costs of achieving agreement internationally; if bringing the relevant domestic constituencies on board is difficult, assembling the support of different national constituencies is likely to be more difficult still.

Attempts to reconstruct the international monetary system—at Genoa in 1922, in London in 1933, at Bretton Woods in 1944, in Europe in the 1970s—have generally sought to establish systems of pegged but adjustable rates or currency bands. Recently, however, policymakers' attention has turned, especially in Europe, to the goal of fixing exchange rates once and for all.

22. See Bruno (1993); Corden (1993); and references cited therein.

23. This view that credible policy reforms will induce immediate changes in behavior on the part of wage and price setters assumes not only forward-looking rational expectations but the absence of nominal inertia attributable to long-term contracts. This is a relatively plausible assumption for inflation-prone economies.

24. The seminal model of balance-of-payments crises is Krugman (1979). For variations on this theme, see Flood and Garber (1984a).

A Pegged-Rate System

The arrangement adopted at Bretton Woods is prototypical of pegged exchange rate systems.[25] Under the terms of the Bretton Woods Agreement, countries agreed to declare official parities against gold or the dollar, to hold their exchange rates within 1 percent of those parities, and to change their parities only in the event of specific circumstances, referred to as a "fundamental disequilibrium."

How does an international agreement like that signed at Bretton Woods differ from a set of unilateral pegs? Under an international agreement, each participant can expect to receive support from the others. In turn, participating countries are expected to take positive steps and to refrain from certain actions in order to maintain their good standing. Under the Bretton Woods Agreement, for example, countries seeking to defend their exchange rates could draw credits from the IMF, initially without restriction and then subject to increasingly stringent conditions.

This feature of the Bretton Woods System, which has its counterpart in other pegged-rate systems, can be thought of as an insurance policy. Each country pays premiums in normal times, providing a pool of resources upon which it can draw when experiencing a crisis. These resources reduce the cost of defending the exchange rate; assuming that different currencies weaken at different times (which is necessarily the case when currencies are pegged to one another rather than to a nonmonetary numeraire like gold), mutual insurance allows the whole set of rates to be defended at lower cost than would be entailed by the maintenance of unilateral pegs.

Insurance is notorious for the moral hazard problems it creates. The IMF, like any insurance company, was therefore vested with responsibility for monitoring member countries and warning those whose actions heightened the danger of a crisis that they might not qualify for indemnification. It was to require of such countries the adoption of corrective policies and to monitor their implementa-

25. Exchange rate experience under the Bretton Woods System is analyzed in more detail in chapter 4. Here I provide only enough detail to illustrate the features of pegged-rate systems and to show how they differ from unilateral pegs.

tion. Changes in central parities were to be undertaken only with the prior approval of the Fund.[26]

A System of Target Zones

Systems of exchange rate target zones are broadly similar to systems of pegged but adjustable rates. As with unilateral target zones, the width of the zone need not be announced. In 1987, for example, the finance ministers of the G-7 countries agreed at the Louvre meeting to establish a set of "reference values" for the dollar and other currencies "around current levels" but declined to reveal the width of the reference range.[27] According to Funabashi, they agreed to a narrow margin of plus or minus 2.5 percent, after which intervention would be called for on a voluntary basis, and a wider band of plus or minus 5 percent, at which point concerted intervention would be obligatory.[28]

Alternatively, the reference range or band width can be announced by the parties to the agreement, as in the case of the Exchange Rate Mechanism (ERM) of the EMS. In return for declaring a central rate and agreeing to other restrictions (devaluing only with the unanimous consent of member countries, for example), ERM participants are entitled to draw on the system's Very Short-Term Financing Facility and to receive support from their partners.[29]

Should participating countries announce a central parity and band width for each participant, as do the members of the ERM, or should they attempt to keep the particulars of the band secret, as did the industrial countries at the Louvre? An implicit band avoids creating focal points for speculation. If currency traders do not know the bottom of the band, they will be unsure at what point the authorities will attempt to keep the rate from falling further and hence at what point capital gains will be available in the event that the measures

26. The question of whether the IMF adequately carried out these responsibilities is at the heart of the debate over the collapse of the Bretton Woods System. These issues come in for further discussion in chapter 4.

27. These phrases from the subsequent communiqué are cited in Frankel (1994). Although officials denied the existence of quantitative target ranges, subsequent research suggests that they in fact set an explicit reference range; see Funabashi (1988, pp. 183–87).

28. See Funabashi (1988). Although these band widths were not announced, they were widely understood to exist. Kenen (1988) provides evidence from press commentary.

29. For details see Ungerer and others (1986); Giavazzi and Giovannini (1989).

taken by the authorities fail. An explicit band, on the other hand, provides an unambiguous signal of the authorities' commitment to stabilizing the exchange rate and should therefore enjoy greater credibility. By providing an explicit statement of the point at which the authorities are prepared to prevent the exchange rate from moving further, it is more likely to give rise to the "honeymoon" effect that is one of the principal advantages of a target zone.

Monetary Union

In a monetary union, the pursuit of a common monetary policy is guaranteed by a transnational entity to which control of the participating countries' monetary policies is assigned.[30] Thus the Maastricht Treaty, the European Union's framework for monetary union, provides for the establishment of a European Central Bank (ECB) responsible for the monetary policies of the participating countries. The credibility problem can be solved by issuing a single currency that circulates in all participating countries and by withdrawing national currencies from circulation. By raising the cost of quitting the union, this institutional exit barrier enhances the credibility of countries' commitment to participate.[31]

If a monetary union is such an effective solution to the exchange rate problem, why then are so few such unions observed? An obvious answer is that monetary union represents one extremity of the continuum between the stability provided by fixed rates and the policy autonomy enjoyed under floating. Having renounced the option of varying the exchange rate and pursuing an independent monetary policy, members of a monetary union may find them-

---

30. Here I concentrate on comparisons between monetary union and other exchange rate arrangements in the steady state. The transition to monetary union opens up other issues, some of which are addressed in chapter 7.

31. The authors of the Delors Report recognized the importance of a single currency as an institutional exit barrier; see Committee for the Study of Economic and Monetary Union (1989). The Maastricht Treaty does not require the ECB to issue a single currency and remove national currencies from circulation upon the inauguration of monetary union, however. Until this is done, the ECB would exchange the currencies of the participating countries for one another at par. Although monetary union will increase the costs of exit, it may not raise them to prohibitive levels. There are examples of monetary unions that have broken up; see Cohen (1993). Similarly, a decision in 1993 by the German Constitutional Court appears to leave open the possibility that the Federal Republic of Germany might opt to leave the European Monetary Union after joining.

selves constrained in responding to national macroeconomic shocks. The absence of exchange risk, together with a high degree of financial market integration, implies that the same level of interest rates must prevail in all participating countries; hence it will no longer be possible to use monetary policy to vary those rates in response to changes in local economic conditions. Stabilization may be hamstrung.[32]

Another reason that one observes so few monetary unions among sovereign nations is the questions of governance they raise. How should policy be formulated—by majority rule in a one-country, one-vote system, or by weighted voting in which weights are proportional to national populations? Should each nation possess veto power over decisions, or should members of the board of the union-wide central bank not have national affiliations at all?

Since a union-wide central bank can, by definition, run only one monetary policy, its policy necessarily matches the interests of some member countries more closely than those of others. What then supports the continued participation of countries with divergent policy preferences? Perhaps the efficiency advantages of a single currency outweigh the costs associated with loss of monetary independence. Alternatively monetary union may be part of a larger political bargain in which a country agrees to monetary unification, which is not in its self-interest when taken in isolation, in return for other political or economic concessions.[33] Or monetary union may be imposed by a dominant country on its subordinate partners by force or intimidation.

---

32. *May* is a weaker word than *will*. There are at least three qualifications to the argument. First, monetary-cum-interest-rate policy may not be an effective response to cyclical disturbances, especially if real wages are impervious to price level changes. If so, sacrificing the monetary instrument will be costless. Second, even if monetary instruments are useful, a common, union-wide monetary policy could suffice if the nations joined together in the monetary union experience similar disturbances. Third, forsaking monetary independence will be less costly when there exist other instruments, such as national fiscal policy and intergovernmental transfers, to take up the slack. I return to these issues in chapter 6.

33. Thus Germany is said to have agreed to monetary union at Maastricht in return for an expanded foreign policy role in the context of a European foreign policy. For elaboration of this argument, see Garrett (1993); Martin (1993); Eichengreen and Frieden (1993). This viewpoint suggests that, until other parts of the world achieve a degree of political integration comparable to that of the European Community, equally ambitious attempts at monetary unification are unlikely to be observed.

Summary

There would appear to be no shortage of international monetary options from which countries can choose (although I suggest subsequently that the range of feasible options is more limited than the preceding menu suggests). Countries may proceed unilaterally, selecting the international monetary arrangement that is optimal from the national point of view, taking the decisions of other nations as given. Or they may harmonize their decisions in order to coordinate on a superior solution. Either way it is necessary to identify the characteristics of a desirable international monetary system. It is to this task that the next chapter turns.

Chapter 3

Prerequisites for International Monetary Stability

W^{HAT} is meant by a successful exchange rate policy or a satisfactory international monetary system? In addressing this question it is important to avoid the tendency to contrast the perceived shortcomings of the prevailing regime with an idealization of the alternatives. In an era of floating, there is a tendency to associate a smoothly functioning international monetary regime with exchange rate stability. And when exchange rates are fixed, there is an analogous tendency to contrast the shortcomings of the existing system with an idealization of the alternative, in this case models of smoothly adjusting floating rates.

These tendencies reflect a simple verity: fixed and flexible exchange rates both have advantages. Fixed rates minimize the disruptions caused by exchange rate volatility and check the more erratic tendencies of policymakers. Flexible rates provide scope for policy initiatives to insulate the economy from disturbances. Successful exchange rate arrangements traditionally are those that have succeeded in combining the advantages of both.

International monetary arrangements with these features all share three characteristics: an ability to effect relative price adjustments, compatibility with the pursuit of robust monetary policies, and capacity to contain market pressures.[1] A system with the capacity to effect relative price adjustments is able to accommodate disturbances. Either the exchange rate itself provides this capacity or substitutes exist for this function of exchange rate changes. A system with this charac-

---

1. This taxonomy builds on Eichengreen and Wyplosz (1993), although I develop it differently here.

teristic thus delivers the main advantages of flexible rates. The pursuit of robust monetary rules and the capacity to contain market pressures are means of limiting exchange rate volatility. They make it possible to stabilize exchange rates at an acceptable cost. A system with these characteristics therefore also delivers the main advantages of fixed rates.

Capacity to Effect Relative Price Adjustments

The disturbances that are most difficult for any economy to accommodate require changes in a large number of prices. Events abroad that reduce the demand for U.S. exports, for example, require a fall in the relative price of the traded goods that the U.S. produces in order to sustain demand for them and prevent the emergence of unemployment and balance-of-payments problems. When exchange rate changes are precluded, this response must occur through the synchronous adjustment of individual wages and prices. But if some prices are slow to respond, output losses and balance-of-payments problems can result. Exchange rate changes may avert these losses by altering many prices at once. This is the "daylight savings time" argument for adjustable rates.

Under a system of fixed rates (insofar as such a thing is possible short of monetary unification), the burden of adjustment falls on domestic prices. Under pegged but adjustable rates, easily accommodated shocks are absorbed through adjustments in prices, whereas exceptional ones may occasion exchange rate changes.

This perspective suggests that a satisfactory international monetary system requires a high degree of exchange rate flexibility when domestic currency prices and costs are slow to adjust.[2] When prices are inflexible downward, a negative demand disturbance will produce unemployment rather than deflation, and an exchange rate change that allows the authorities to pursue demand management policies to offset the disturbance will be exceptionally valuable. Thus when disturbances requiring relative price adjustments are frequent and large, the advantages of exchange rate flexibility are enhanced.

2. This is one of the messages of the literature on optimum currency areas discussed in chapter 6.

That exchange rates can be used to facilitate adjustment is most obvious under floating. But the same is true of the systems of pegged exchange rates that have prevailed over the last one hundred years. All such systems have featured escape clauses permitting pegged rates to be changed in the event of exceptional shocks.[3] The theory of escape clauses emphasizes that "fixed" rates can be changed without undermining the authorities' commitment to exchange rate stability if such changes are initiated only in response to exceptional shocks that are directly observable or otherwise independently verifiable and if those shocks are not initiated by the authorities themselves.[4] If these conditions are met, then the costs of maintaining exchange rate stability should be relatively low. When no exceptional shock justifying a permanent depreciation has been observed, market participants, when they see the exchange rate weakening, will expect the authorities to intervene in its support. Traders will purchase the currency in anticipation of those measures of support, strengthening the rate without the need for actual intervention. The costs of stabilizing the exchange rate will be minimized. In the event of an exceptional shock requiring far-reaching adjustment, however, the authorities will be able to alter that rate without undermining the credibility of their commitment to defending it in normal times.

In theory, then, an escape clause permitting exchange rate changes in the event of exceptional shocks should not interfere with the ability to reap the benefits of exchange rate stability. Whether resort to an escape clause is feasible in practice, when exceptional exogenous shocks are difficult to distinguish from other disturbances, is a more difficult question, as I now explain.

Compatibility with the Adherence to Robust Monetary Rules

If the contingencies triggering exceptional exchange rate changes are not independently verifiable and clearly exogenous with respect to the authorities' actions, an exchange rate escape clause will lack

3. Even under the classical gold standard, as we shall see in chapter 4, there was provision for suspending gold convertibility and allowing the exchange rate to depreciate in the event of exceptional shocks.

4. On the theory of escape clauses, see Grossman and van Huyck (1988); De Kock and Grilli (1989); Flood and Isard (1989); Giovannini (1993).

credibility.[5] Observers may dismiss the central bank's assurances that the exchange rate's fluctuation is temporary and reversible, since no readily observable, exogenous shock triggering the escape clause has occurred. They may suspect the authorities of manipulating the rate under cover of their contingent rule, manufacturing the relevant disturbance, or claiming that it has occurred when it has not. The movement of the rate to the edge of its fluctuation band will not elicit stabilizing speculation. Even worse, the existence of an escape clause may be destabilizing. Imagine that the authorities vow to devalue only when circumstances are sufficiently bad. If the markets expect that the authorities are inclined to manufacture or simply to announce unverifiable circumstances justifying a devaluation, they will sell the currency in anticipation, increasing the pressure on the authorities to the point that the latter are forced to respond as expected. In the limit, this set of circumstances renders the escape clause and exchange rate stability incompatible, requiring the authorities to choose between them.[6]

Private information and moral hazard problems thereby handicap efforts to construct hybrid systems combining the advantages of fixed and flexible rates. They create difficulties for all systems in which policy is framed in terms of an exchange rate target, from pegged but adjustable rates to target zones with realignment options and soft buffers to preannounced crawling pegs.

A solution is for the government to acquire a reputation for defending its currency peg. Even if the markets are incapable of verifying on short notice whether an exceptional exogenous disturbance justifying a change in the exchange rate peg has occurred, as long as the government possesses a reputation for defending the rate in the event of all but exceptional exogenous shocks, it will pay for currency traders to bet that this is what the authorities will do when the exchange rate weakens. Market participants may not possess all the information available to the Dutch government when it decides whether or not to alter the guilder–deutsche mark exchange rate, but the reputation the Netherlands Central Bank has acquired from years of successfully pegging the guilder to the deutsche mark nonetheless induces traders to speculate in stabilizing ways. The fact that the

5. These private information and moral hazard problems are respectively emphasized by Canzoneri (1985); Obstfeld (1991).

6. This is an implication of the model developed by Obstfeld (1991).

escape clause exists (that the Netherlands can still alter the guilder price of the deutsche mark) is thereby reconciled with exchange rate stability.

To acquire this reputation, the authorities must pursue a consistent policy (in the present example, pegging the exchange rate to the deutsche mark) in the face of all but the most exceptional shocks. Whether an exceptional shock cited by the authorities as justification for an exchange rate adjustment has really occurred and is exogenous with respect to the government's actions can generally be verified with the passage of time and the accumulation of evidence from successive episodes. By behaving over time in a consistent manner, the authorities can acquire the reputation needed to support the smooth operation of an exchange rate escape clause. This is how the stability of pegged but occasionally adjustable exchange rates under the classical gold standard is best understood.

Some argue that credibility can also be acquired by making the central bank independent in order to insulate it from political pressures. Independence will not in general suffice, however, for the central bank may retain an incentive to behave in time-inconsistent ways. Imagine a central bank playing a noncooperative game with the domestic fiscal authority. In deciding whether to use the inflation tax and to disregard its exchange rate commitment in order to help finance the government's deficit, an optimizing central bank will equate at the margin the costs of revenues raised with distortionary taxes and seigniorage.[7] Faced with a government engaged in high levels of spending and levying highly distortionary taxes, an independent central banker possessing discretion will rationally create additional inflation. Central banks may state their intention of maintaining price and exchange rate stability and of refusing to monetize additional budget deficits; but when such deficits arise, the monetary authorities, upon solving the optimal taxation problem, will prefer to equate on the margin the deadweight loss of distortionary taxes and inflation, violating their preannounced rule. This knowledge may then encourage their fiscal counterparts to run excessive deficits. The problem of time inconsistency thereby limits the ability of even an independent central bank to commit credibly to a monetary policy consistent with exchange rate stabilization.

---

7. This is known as the Ramsey-Phelps optimal taxation problem. The example of this paragraph is drawn from Canzoneri and Diba (1991). On the economics of seigniorage and monetary unification, see also Canzoneri and Rogers (1990).

Central bank independence by itself will not solve the problem. It must be buttressed directly by a rule requiring the monetary authorities to adhere to a certain policy, or indirectly by a rule requiring the fiscal authorities to do so. An example of the former is currency board arrangements, and an instance of the latter is the "excessive deficits procedures" of the European Union's Maastricht Treaty on Economic and Monetary Union.[8]

Simply invoking rules as a source of credibility assumes a solution to the problem. If discretionary policy lacks credibility, in other words, what lends credibility to the rule? When the time for time inconsistency comes, those with discretion over the rules will have the same incentive to violate them as discretionary policymakers have to exercise their discretion.[9] A solution to this problem is to establish institutions that impose costs on those violating the rules. For example, countries joining the International Monetary Fund (IMF) after World War II signed the IMF Articles of Agreement, committing to declare par values for their currencies and to hold their exchange rates within narrow bands. The sanction was that countries failing to unify their currencies, declare par values, and defend them would lose access to Fund resources.[10] European governments ratified the Maastricht Treaty, an international agreement under which they incur fines in the event that they pursue certain macroeconomic practices. Another device is to link the commitment to cooperate in managing bilateral exchange rates to another issue, say, a common foreign policy.[11]

---

8. These procedures limit the debts and deficits that states can run when seeking to qualify for membership in the European monetary union and provide sanctions to be applied to members that subsequently run "excessive" debts and deficits. For details see Buiter, Corsetti, and Roubini (1993).

9. "Self-imposed rules tend to lose their force, and thus their influence on credibility, as soon as they come into conflict with other policy goals," as Kenen (1988, p. 19) puts the point.

10. In practice, countries that failed to defend their par values were not always denied access to Fund resources.

11. This is the rationale for Germany's commitment to European monetary unification, at least according to certain observers. For further discussion, see chapter 6. More generally, these arguments are an application of the literature on institutions as a solution to time-consistency problems; see North (1993). They are also the message of the literature on issue linkage in international politics, where linkage can be used to create hostages; see Tollison and Willet (1979).

All these examples are ways for governments to tie themselves to the mast—to create extra costs for themselves if they fail to adhere to the relevant policies. The more efficiently the parties to the agreement monitor compliance and the more vigorously they respond to violations, the greater will be the added credibility. This approach provides an argument for international monetary reform at the systemic level in preference to unilateral national initiatives, and for international institutions to monitor compliance with the relevant rules. Both sorts of measures could help governments credibly commit to the pursuit of robust monetary policies.

Capacity to Contain Market Pressures

The third characteristic of a smoothly operating exchange rate system is the capacity to contain market pressures. As an asset price, a freely floating exchange rate will fluctuate in response to new information. When they are offered a one-way bet (as will tend to be the case when the authorities attempt to operate a system of pegged but adjustable rates or exchange rate target zones), currency traders may bet heavily against the official position on even the off-chance that the authorities have a limited capacity to defend it. To prevent these pressures from destabilizing the exchange rate and even the entire exchange rate system, the authorities must possess the means for containing market pressures.

Two Types of Market Pressures

Not all market pressures are to be resisted. Here it is useful to distinguish two kinds of balance-of-payments crises. In the seminal model of Krugman, a crisis occurs because the authorities adopt monetary and fiscal policies fundamentally incompatible with the currency peg. Budget deficits are too large, the monetization of fiscal deficits is too rapid, and reserve losses are too great for the authorities to continue resisting pressure to devalue.[12] The capacity to contain market pressures temporarily may be useful to provide the breathing space needed to organize an orderly realignment and preserve a system of pegged but

12. See Krugman (1979).

adjustable exchange rates, but it would be silly to attempt to resist that pressure indefinitely, given underlying policies.

A second class of models, due to Flood and Garber and Obstfeld, suggests that there are circumstances under which speculative attacks on pegged exchange rates can occur and succeed without any imbalance in underlying policies.[13] In the absence of an attack, the exchange rate peg can be maintained indefinitely. Thus, these models do not assume the fiscal deficits and excessively expansionary monetary policies that provoke the attack in the Krugman model. If and only if an attack occurs, however, the authorities will modify policy in a more expansionary direction.[14] Knowing that policy will be modified in the event of an attack, speculators have an incentive to undertake one, since they reap capital gains once the expansionary shift induces a depreciation.[15] Thus if the authorities have the capacity to resist this attack, they can maintain exchange rate stability indefinitely. The greater their capacity to resist market pressures, the more stable will be the exchange rate system.

An example is useful for illustrating the point. Consider the choice confronting European Union member states attempting to qualify for participation in the monetary union. The Maastricht Treaty makes two years of exchange rate stability a precondition for participation.[16] Even if a country has its domestic financial house in order and its government is willing to trade austerity now for a ticket to participate in the monetary union later, an exchange market crisis that forces the country to devalue its currency and abandon its Exchange Rate

13. See Flood and Garber (1984b); and Obstfeld (1986). The literature that underlies the following discussion is reviewed by Agenor, Bhandari, and Flood (1992); Obstfeld (1994).

14. In chapter 5, I offer examples designed to illustrate circumstances under which it may be rational for a government to behave in this way.

15. This begs the question of what leads foreign exchange traders to mobilize against a currency at a particular time. The theoretical literature assumes identical agents—that is, foreign exchange traders all react simultaneously. Alternatively, one could assume that individual traders are not liquidity constrained, so that any one is able to borrow to the extent required to undertake the attack. Another assumption is that traders watch the activities of a particularly prominent market participant and respond in kind; thus the actions and statements of the well-known currency speculator George Soros figured prominently in accounts of the 1992 European currency crisis.

16. More precisely, exchange rates must remain within their normal European Monetary System fluctuation bands without severe tensions.

Mechanism peg may still disqualify it from early participation. If it no longer qualifies for the monetary union, its government has no remaining incentive to continue pursuing the policies of austerity required to gain entry. It is likely therefore to switch to a more accommodating monetary and fiscal stance. Even if in the absence of a speculative attack there is no problem with fundamentals, either current or future, once an attack occurs the government has an incentive to modify policy in a more accommodating direction, validating speculators' expectations of capital gains. In this setting, a speculative attack can be self-fulfilling.

Instruments for Containing Market Pressures

Three instruments are generally available for containing market pressures. The first is interest rates. The authorities can raise yields on domestic-currency-denominated assets to whatever heights are required to render investors indifferent as to whether they hold them or hold foreign exchange. Since exchange rate changes occurring in short order offer very large capital gains to currency traders who sell their domestic-currency-denominated assets just prior to devaluation and buy them back immediately thereafter, rendering those traders indifferent may require raising interest rates to very high levels. A 10 percent devaluation expected to occur in ten days with 90 percent probability offers risk-neutral investors an expected annualized return of nearly 500 percent. To defend a currency peg it may be necessary to raise interest rates to that level.[17]

Alternatively, the government can apply capital controls. Controls on short-term capital movements need not be impermeable in order to provide insulation from market pressures. If it costs 5 percent of principal to evade controls, speculators will be indifferent to the choice between holding domestic- and foreign-currency-denominated assets even if they anticipate a 10 percent devaluation.[18]

---

17. As noted in chapter 2, that this is more than a hypothetical case is evident in the experience of Sweden in the autumn of 1992, when the Riksbank raised its marginal lending rate to 500 percent in an attempt to fend off a speculative attack.

18. This assumes that evading the controls costs 10 percent on a round trip.

Figure 3-1. *Effect of Capital Controls on Interest Rates for Two European Countries, Selected Years, 1980–93*

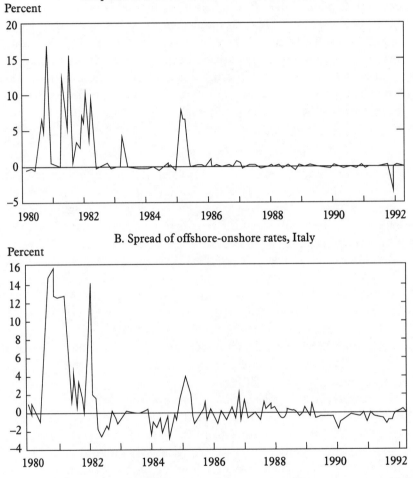

A. Spread of offshore-onshore interbank rates, France

Percent

B. Spread of offshore-onshore rates, Italy

Percent

Source: Data Resources, Inc., database.

Figure 3-1 shows how much difference controls made for the level of interest rates in two European countries in the 1980s. The onshore-offshore interest differential for France and Italy approached 20 percent during periods of intense speculative pressure. The implication is that the authorities in these countries had to raise interest rates by 20 percentage points less than they would have had to otherwise to render domestic investors indifferent to the choice between holding domestic and foreign assets.[19]

Finally other countries participating in the international arrangement can support the currency under attack. In terms of the analogy developed in chapter 2, international cooperation serves as insurance: each country pays insurance premiums by contributing to collective support of other currencies; when its own currency shows signs of instability, it receives the support of its foreign counterparts. The interest rate increases or impediments to international capital mobility that must be applied by the country whose currency is under attack are thereby moderated, reducing the costs of defense. As we shall see in chapter 4, cooperation in support of particular currencies, whether organized via ad hoc arrangements between central banks and governments, through the facilities of an international organization like the IMF, or under the provisions of an automatic credit line like the Very Short-Term Financing Facility of the European Monetary System, has been a feature of all durable international monetary systems.

These prerequisites for international monetary stability have been provided under a variety of different institutional arrangements. The problem posed by deep integration is that accompanying changes in technology, politics, and market structures may render their provision increasingly difficult. It may be possible only under a very limited set of international monetary arrangements.

Summary

A viable international monetary system must satisfy three conditions. First, it must provide a means for effecting changes in relative prices. Even if exchange rates are normally pegged, there must be allowance for them to change in response to disturbances requiring relative price shifts too large to be easily accommodated by decentralized markets, or there must exist a substitute for the otherwise obligatory exchange rate movements. Second, robust monetary rules must

19. The fact that domestic-currency-denominated assets already outside the country could be traded on terms free of capital controls is not relevant here. The issue is to what extent the yields on domestic-currency-denominated assets had to be raised to prevent additional quantities from flowing out of the country. The offshore rate can be taken as an indicator of the product of the expected devaluation magnitude and expected devaluation probability.

be pursued to lend credibility to the rates that prevail in the absence of exceptional shocks. Countries may unilaterally earn a reputation for adhering to such rules, or they may create international institutions to monitor compliance and levy sanctions against violators. Finally, provision must be made for containing market pressures in the event of uncertainty about the policy rule followed by the authorities; options for doing so include capital controls and foreign support.

Have all international monetary systems that operated successfully for extended periods satisfied these conditions? Can the demise of those systems be understood in terms of their failure ultimately to meet one or more of them? The next chapter attempts to answer these questions.

Chapter 4

Evidence from the Historical Record

I NOW review the history of the international monetary system in light of the concepts developed in chapter 3. This review provides concrete illustrations of the importance for the operation of viable international monetary arrangements of the ability to effect relative price changes, of the credible pursuit of robust monetary rules, and of the capacity to contain market pressures. It shows how the ability of particular international monetary arrangements to meet these conditions helps to explain their success and how their eventual failure to do so accounts for their ultimate demise. In anticipation of chapter 5, it suggests that the circumstances that permitted these three conditions to be met in the past by systems of pegged rates will no longer be present in the future.

The Classical Gold Standard

Between 1880 and 1913 the industrial nations maintained the free convertibility of domestic currency into gold at a fixed price. Through arbitrage in international gold markets, these policies yielded stable exchange rates. As long as external convertibility was maintained and there were no impediments to international gold shipments, exchange rates could not vary by more than the gold points (a band around the ratio of domestic and foreign gold prices defined by the costs of shipping and insuring gold).[1]

1. Exchange rates under the gold standard fluctuated, in other words, within a target zone whose limits were defined by the gold points. Along with these pecuniary costs, there was also the opportunity cost of the funds devoted to arbitrage (funds invested in gold did not earn interest for the period the gold was in transit).

Yet the classical gold standard does not seem, at least superficially, to have satisfied the prerequisites for a smoothly functioning international monetary system. Exchange rates were stabilized for extended periods without obvious recourse to capital controls or international support. Wages and prices were far from flexible; recent historical studies lend little support to the notion that the nineteenth century was an era of perfectly flexible markets.[2]

From this perspective, the smooth operation of the gold standard is a mystery of the highest order. Fortunately, recent research goes a long way toward solving it. One strand emphasizes the existence and operation of escape clauses.[3] Countries buffeted by exceptional disturbances could and did suspend gold convertibility temporarily to facilitate adjustment without sacrificing credibility. The prototypical example of an exceptional disturbance is a war. Thus Britain was able to suspend convertibility during the French wars without undermining the credibility of its commitment to gold, as was the United States during its Civil War. The escape clause could also be invoked in response to purely financial disturbances, as with the 1847 suspension by the Bank of England. The exceptional nature of the crisis and the temporary nature of the suspension were signaled by an emergency waiver of the Bank Act of 1844 issued by the Chancellor of the Exchequer and validated by Parliament's passage of a special law.

What rendered credible the claim that suspensions were temporary? In Europe the commitment to gold convertibility was the very cornerstone of policy. In the countries at the center of the system—Britain, France, and Germany—there was no doubt, barring the most exceptional circumstances, that the authorities would take whatever steps were needed to defend the central bank's gold reserves, to maintain the convertibility of the currency, and to restore convertibility at the previous rate if it proved necessary to suspend it temporarily. This was the epitome of a robust monetary rule.

2. Structured labor markets limited the flexibility of wages, both over time and across workers, even prior to widespread trade unionism and the rise of internal labor markets. Comparisons of wage flexibility for pre–World War I and interwar Britain do not provide strong evidence of a secular decline in labor market flexibility. See Hatton (1988). A recent study of this subject by Obstfeld concludes that "Nominal prices in most industrial countries display symptoms of stickiness even in the gold standard period. Nominal price inflexibility seems to have increased after World War II, but the evidence favoring this hypothesis is not overwhelming, and the extent of the increase may not be large" (1993, p. 246).

3. See in particular Bordo and Kydland (1992); Giovannini (1993).

Further enhancing the credibility of the commitment to convertibility was the fact that the connections between monetary policy and the domestic economy remained incompletely understood. As long as there was no properly articulated theory of the relationship between central bank policy and the level of unemployment, observers could disagree about whether the level of interest rates was damaging employment prospects; their disagreement neutralized the pressure that might have otherwise been brought to bear to modify monetary policy. The credibility of governments' commitment to convertibility was enhanced by the fact that those who suffered most from unemployment were in no position to make their objections felt. In most countries, the right to vote was limited to men of property; women were still denied the vote virtually everywhere. Labor parties representing working men were in their formative years. The working man at risk of unemployment when the central bank raised interest rates had little opportunity to voice his objections, much less to expel from office the government and central bankers responsible for the policy.

Chapter 3 described how fiscal rules can buttress the credibility of an exchange rate commitment. The argument applies to the fiscal norms under which governments functioned at the gold standard's European core. Public spending ratios were low. Budgets were balanced. Governments "generally abided by a balanced budget objective, which could be regarded, in effect, as representing the required fiscal constraint on national policies."[4]

For all these reasons, a negative disturbance to a country's balance of payments rarely weakened the exchange rate to the point where painfully large interest rate increases had to take place. Instead the exchange rate's weakness was offset by capital inflows prompted by the expectation that the authorities would do what was required to stabilize it. This fact limited the distress caused by those necessary steps.

Experience was very different at the periphery of the gold standard system. Latin American countries also suspended convertibility and allowed their currencies to depreciate when the supply of foreign

---

4. Goodhart (1992, p. 192). Bloomfield (1959, p. 20) makes the same point: "Central banks also operated within the framework of economies where the public sector was in general only a relatively small one, where fiscal policy and debt management policy in their modern sense were virtually unknown, and where government budgets were for the most part in balance."

capital or the demand for exports was disrupted. There, however, the credibility of the commitment to gold convertibility did not always survive intact. Though suspensions of convertibility were character-ized as temporary, this did not always turn out to be the case.

The explanation for the contrast lies in differences, compared to Europe, in the credibility and robustness of the monetary regime and in the capacity for containing market pressures.[5] In the United States, agricultural debtors and silver mining interests formed a powerful coalition opposed to deflation and advocating modification of the monetary standard to allow for the coinage of silver.[6] Such groups existed in Europe as well, but in the United States they had better access to the political process because of universal male suffrage. Throughout Latin America, as in the United States, depreciation was welcomed by landowners with fixed mortgage obligations and export-ers wishing to enhance their competitive position internationally. As in the United States, the two groups were often one and the same. And as in the United States, their ranks were swelled by mining interests favoring the coinage of silver.

Nor did adherence to strict fiscal norms buttress the credibility of the exchange rate commitment at the periphery of the gold standard system. Latin American countries repeatedly failed to control their fiscal policies, leading to monetization of budget deficits, the suspen-sion of gold convertibility, and currency depreciation. Even in the United States, fiscal imbalances threatened the commitment to the exchange rate peg in the 1890s.[7]

Thus most countries of the Western Hemisphere did not have unblemished reputations for obeying robust monetary rules, prompt-ing questions about their commitment to the prevailing exchange rate. Latin American countries were repeatedly forced to abandon the gold standard involuntarily in the final decades of the nineteenth century. The same was nearly true of the United States during the run-up to the 1896 presidential campaign, in which William Jennings

5. Countries specializing in the production of primary products also suffered larger terms-of-trade shocks than the more diversified industrial economies, which strained their capacity to maintain their exchange rate pegs. This point is emphasized by Bordo (1993b) and Eichengreen (1992a).

6. Frieden (1991) provides evidence that these groups would have benefited from, and therefore favored, the devaluation of the dollar that would have followed from the extensive coinage of silver.

7. See Garber and Grilli (1986).

Bryan made the exchange rate a central issue.[8] In the same way that robust monetary rules and well-defined escape clauses facilitated the functioning of the classical gold standard at its European center, at its periphery their absence disrupted its operation.

The gold standard also required means of containing market pressures. Such pressures could be intense: prior to 1914 the volume of international capital flows—long- and short-term alike— reached impressive heights.[9] Countries did not deploy capital controls to insulate themselves from speculative pressures; instead they utilized the so-called "gold devices" to widen the band within which their bilateral exchange rates could float. Recall that fluctuation bands for exchange rates under the gold standard were given by the gold points (the wedge created for gold market arbitrage by the costs of insurance and shipping). Measures widening this band could relieve the pressure on the authorities to raise interest rates in response to a capital outflow that weakened the exchange rate. Central banks might raise buying and selling prices for gold bars or redeem notes only for worn and clipped gold coin, measures tantamount to depreciation.[10] They might discourage gold exports by redeeming notes only at the central bank's head office. Some could legally redeem their notes either in gold coin or in silver pieces whose market value was less than their face value, another practice tantamount to a temporary suspension.

The other means of coping with market pressures was international support. International cooperation was episodic, but instances in which it occurred were precisely those in which the system's anchor currencies came under attack. Central banks discounted bills on behalf of the affected country or lent gold to its monetary authority. The most famous such instance was the 1890 Baring Crisis, when the Bank of England was faced with the insolvency of a major British bank, Baring Brothers, which had extended bad loans to the government of Argentina. The Bank of England borrowed £3 million of gold from the Bank of France and

8. See Eichengreen (forthcoming). In comparing the dollar exchange rate with those of the German mark and the French franc, Giovannini (1993) concludes that capital showed less of a tendency to flow in stabilizing directions in the U.S. case.

9. See Bloomfield (1968). This is true even by late twentieth-century standards: see Bayoumi (1990); Eichengreen (1991b); Obstfeld (forthcoming).

10. For details see Morgenstern (1959), p. 441.

obtained a pledge of £1.5 million of gold coin from Russia.[11] With the help of this foreign support, the crisis was averted, and sterling's gold standard survived intact.

This kind of regime-preserving cooperation was repeated in 1895, when a consortium of European banks, with the encouragement of their governments, helped defend the U.S. gold standard.[12] In 1898 the Reichsbank and German commercial banks obtained assistance from the Bank of England and the Bank of France. In 1906 and 1907 the Bank of England, confronted with another financial crisis, again obtained support from the Bank of France and, in addition, from the Reichsbank. The Russian State Bank shipped gold to Berlin to replenish the Reichsbank's reserves. In 1909 and 1910 the Bank of France again discounted British bills, making gold available to London. Smaller European countries such as Belgium, Norway, and Sweden also borrowed reserves from foreign central banks and governments. This would appear to be a clear instance of the kind of risk-pooling arrangements described in the preceding chapter.

Significantly, regime-preserving cooperation was largely limited to the gold standard's European core and on occasion the United States.[13] Smaller, less-developed countries of the periphery did not receive comparable support. Their capacity to contain market pressures was therefore more limited.

The success of the classical gold standard at its European center is thus explicable in terms of the prerequisites for a viable international monetary system identified in chapter 3. The absence of those prerequisites and the consequent instability of the gold standard at the periphery offer further proof by counterexample.

It is interesting to speculate how long this system would have endured had World War I not intervened. De Cecco argues that by

11. The action was not unprecedented. The Bank of England had borrowed gold from the Bank of France in 1839, through the mediation of the very same Baring Brothers. The Bank of England returned the favor in 1847. The Swedish Riksbank had borrowed several million kroner from the Danish National Bank in 1882. See Eichengreen (1992a, pp. 50–52).

12. The phrase *regime-preserving cooperation* comes from Kenen (1990), who distinguishes it from the continuous cooperation implied by the policy-optimizing approach to international policy coordination.

13. Since the Federal Reserve System had not yet been established, this was not central bank cooperation; it brought together the U.S. Treasury and various European banks. Garber and Grilli (1986) provide an analysis of the Belmont Morgan Syndicate, through which the U.S. gold standard was supported in the early 1890s.

1913 the prewar system was already exhibiting incipient instability. The prewar years were marked by growing consciousness of unemployment, especially in countries like Britain.[14] Authors like Ralph Hawtrey offered theories connecting high interest rates with trade depression.[15] The extent of the franchise was broadened. Such factors intensified pressures to modify the conduct of monetary policy so as to achieve domestic objectives unrelated to maintenance of the exchange rate and challenged the pursuit of robust monetary rules.

Once seeds of doubt were planted about the authorities' commitment to exchange rate stability, resort to the exchange rate escape clause grew problematic. The kind of temporary suspensions of gold convertibility that had been commonplace in prior years were no longer feasible, a fact that made the relative price adjustments associated with exceptional shocks more difficult to effect. International cooperation remained sufficiently extensive that the system survived, but it was not clear that it would suffice in the event of a major disturbance.

Interwar Arrangements

International monetary arrangements between the wars are notorious for their poor performance. This section seeks to explain why.

Floating Exchange Rates

The experience with flexible exchange rates in the first half of the 1920s created an aversion to generalized floating that lingered for half a century. That experience is readily explicable in terms of the absence of robust monetary rules. The entire constellation of forces that had facilitated their pursuit was weakened by World War I. Central banks were subordinated to ministries of finance and budget, limiting

14. In addition, de Cecco (1984) argues that inevitable changes in the composition of the reserve base tended to erode confidence in the system. Insofar as the demand for international reserves to back domestic money supplies expanded faster than the supply of newly mined gold, the latter was supplemented with growing quantities of foreign exchange reserves, thus heightening confidence problems. Eventually, the demand for foreign exchange reserves by central banks would outstrip the gold in the possession of the reserve-currency countries, creating the kind of Triffin Dilemma from which the Bretton Woods System suffered in its later years.

15. See Hawtrey (1913).

their independence. Universal male suffrage, the rise of parliamentary labor parties, and the prominence acquired by the connections between monetary policy and unemployment politicized the policy decisions of central bankers, who retained little insulation. The immediate postwar period was dominated by disputes over economic policy generally, and consistent, robust monetary policies were one casualty of those disagreements. As long as central banks were in thrall to governments, political deadlocks over whose taxes should be raised or whose public programs should be cut ended up in the lap of the monetary authorities, who were forced to print money to reconcile incompatible claims.

The New Gold Standard

This disastrous experience bred its own solution. Financial chaos broke down resistance to fiscal compromise, and inflation weakened opposition to central bank independence. Countries that had endured inflation in the first half of the 1920s stabilized and joined the interwar gold standard already reestablished by countries like Britain and the Netherlands, which had succeeded in restoring their prewar parities. For predictable reasons, however, this new system proved less hardy than its prewar predecessor. Monetary policy remained politicized, especially as long as unemployment remained at high levels. Fiscal policy proved increasingly difficult to subordinate to the pursuit of robust monetary rules. Central banks that raised interest rates to defend the currency came under political pressure from those concerned with the consequences for unemployment.

For political reasons, therefore, the pursuit of robust monetary rules proved not to be feasible. This rendered problematic a recourse to the escape clause feature of the prewar system. In contrast to prevailing practice during the late nineteenth century, governments hesitated to resort to temporary suspensions of convertibility.

Containing market pressures was equally difficult. International support for weak exchange rates proved difficult to arrange: domestic political constraints, international political disputes, and incompatible conceptual frameworks stood in the way. Special interest groups that might be hurt by cooperative adjustments of economic policies were able to stave them off. The dispute over European war debts and German reparations obstructed efforts to cooperate. The incompatible conceptual frameworks employed in various countries prevented policymakers from reaching a common understanding of their economic problems and agreeing on a solution. In 1931 market pressures proved impossible to contain, and the new gold standard broke down.

Managed Floating

International monetary arrangements gradually evolved toward managed floating. Some two dozen countries abandoned the gold standard with Britain's departure in September 1931, and others followed. A few, like the United States, eventually repegged to gold at devalued rates. The vast majority cut the link to gold convertibility once and for all. Rather than letting their currencies float freely, however, governments attempted to influence their movement through foreign exchange intervention. The imposition of capital controls helped them attain this goal.

Still the managed float of the 1930s featured none of the prerequisites for a smoothly functioning international monetary system. Governments shifted from one policy rule to another, casting doubt on their commitment to prevailing exchange rates. The exchange rate risk premium grew significantly.[16] Speculative capital moved in destabilizing directions. Efforts to cooperate in containing market pressures rarely amounted to much.

The 1936 Tripartite Agreement was a first tentative step toward constructing a viable international monetary order. Governments reaffirmed their commitment to cooperate, and exchange rate volatility caused by competitive depreciation was reduced.[17] All this suggests that the Tripartite Agreement mattered. But real progress in reconstructing the international monetary system only gathered momentum after World War II.

Post–World War II Arrangements

The most important of these postwar innovations was the Bretton Woods Agreement.

16. See Eichengreen (1991a).
17. Standard measures of the foreign exchange risk premium suggest that it declined after 1936; see Eichengreen (1992a, chapter 12).

Bretton Woods

The agreement negotiated at Bretton Woods was an effort to reestablish a viable international monetary order. To provide the capacity to undertake relative price adjustments, the Bretton Woods Agreement included an escape clause. Though required to declare par values for their currencies and to maintain them within 1 percent of that value (defined in terms of the July 1, 1944, gold content of the U.S. dollar), signatories were still permitted to alter that par value in the event of a "fundamental disequilibrium." Unfortunately, disagreement between American and British negotiators about how much leeway countries should possess in invoking this provision caused them to leave the term undefined. The stipulation that countries consult with the International Monetary Fund (IMF) and obtain its agreement before devaluing and the possibility that they might become ineligible for Fund resources if they failed to do so can be thought of as attempts to guarantee that the disturbances in response to which exchange rate changes were made were independently verifiable.[18] In practice, however, countries did not always obtain Fund authorization in advance of devaluation. On only one occasion, that of France in 1948, did the Fund treat an exchange rate change as unauthorized. Nothing in the procedures governing changes in par values guaranteed that these would be effected only in response to disequilibria caused by shocks not of a government's own making.

The fact that these procedures did not guarantee that changes in par values would occur only in response to exceptional shocks that were both independently verifiable and not of the authorities' own making left countries hesitant to resort to the escape clause for fear that its utilization would damage their credibility.[19] From this point of view, it is no surprise that devaluations by industrial-country participants in the Bretton Woods System were rare. The only ones of any significance in the 1950s and 1960s were those by France in 1957, 1958, and 1969 and by the United Kingdom in 1967.[20]

The other way of understanding this hesitancy to resort to the escape clause provision of the Bretton Woods Agreement is in terms

18. Dominguez (1993) emphasizes the monitoring and informational roles of the IMF.

19. Britain's unilateral devaluation in 1949 may have had just such a credibility-damaging effect, as argued by Obstfeld (1993).

20. Canada, which maintained a floating exchange rate in the 1950s, might be added to this list.

of the absence of robust monetary rules. Skeptical that governments were adequately committed to the pursuit of robust rules, the markets disregarded official assurances that any weakening of the exchange rate was temporary. Hence the authorities could not afford to allow any weakening at all.

The statement that central banks did not always follow robust monetary rules is a relative one, of course. The robustness of the prevailing monetary rules may have compared unfavorably with that of the gold standard era, when central banks' commitment to exchange rate stability dominated other peacetime objectives and insulation from political pressures was extensive. After World War II, in contrast, monetary policymakers were torn between the desire for exchange rate and price stability on the one hand and Keynesian arguments for policy activism to reduce unemployment and stabilize the business cycle on the other. At the same time the stability of monetary policy—the robustness of the prevailing monetary rules in the present terminology—was impressive compared to that in either the 1920s and 1930s or the years following the breakdown of the Bretton Woods System. Recent research on Bretton Woods suggests that exogenous shifts in monetary policy were relatively uncommon, especially following the restoration of current account convertibility at the end of 1958.[21] An implication is that the success that Bretton Woods enjoyed was due partly to the robustness, limited but significant, that characterized monetary policies.

What accounts for this modest robustness of monetary rules in the heyday of Bretton Woods? Outside the United States and the United Kingdom, the influence of the Keynesian revolution was still weak, and efforts to use monetary policy to manipulate output and employment remained rare.[22] Memory of exchange rate volatility in the first half of the 1920s and of beggar-thy-neighbor devaluations in the

21. Eichenbaum and Evans (1993) report various measures of the magnitude of monetary policy shocks during these years, concluding that they were smaller than in surrounding periods. Bordo (1993b) and Eichengreen (1993a) use a different methodology, due to Blanchard and Quah (1989), to derive estimates of aggregate demand disturbances, to which monetary policy disturbances are one contributor, and find that these were smaller between 1959 and 1970 than in surrounding periods. In my 1993a paper I also show that inflationary monetary policy disturbances were much less persistent than those after 1971.

22. In Germany, for example, the use of monetary policy for stabilization was virtually unknown. See Schonfield (1965); Bordo (1993a). Only following the German stabilization law of the mid-1960s did this situation change.

1930s left governments reluctant to alter monetary policy if doing so meant risking exchange rate stability.

Perhaps the most significant changes in international monetary arrangements achieved at Bretton Woods were those designed to contain market pressures. The agreement provided for an International Monetary Fund to support currencies in distress. Members subscribed quotas one-quarter in gold and three-quarters in their own currency and could draw, subject to conditions, foreign currency in the amount of 125 percent of their quotas. Borrowings were conditional on the pursuit of policies stipulated by the Fund and on repayment of drawings in three to five years. Standby arrangements, whereby member countries could obtain financial assistance from the Fund in advance of difficulties, were introduced in the 1950s. This was not the kind of unlimited support needed to sustain weak currencies indefinitely, but it provided ammunition for countries seeking to counter speculative attacks.

The industrial countries provided one another with additional support through a variety of ad hoc agreements. In 1961 the leading central banks initialed the Basle Agreement, committing to hold one another's currencies and to engage in reciprocal lending. Later that year the London gold pool was established to stem the drain of gold reserves from the United States. In 1962 the industrial countries established swap facilities to provide reciprocal credit lines. This was followed by the General Agreements to Borrow (under which the IMF could borrow from industrial countries with payments surpluses to assist those with deficits), Special Drawing Rights (proposed in 1968 and allocated in 1970), and other devices for increasing the resources that could be made available to central banks in distress. Once again this was not unlimited support; even the sum of these resources did not always suffice to repel the speculative pressures that financial markets could bring to bear, as illustrated by the ultimately unsuccessful efforts to defend sterling. But they could be very important in specific instances: an example is the March 1964 multilateral credit facility, which prevented Italy from having to devalue the lira.

Two implications follow for efforts to understand the operation of the Bretton Woods System. First, the extent of international cooperation in the provision of exchange rate support was one of the key features distinguishing Bretton Woods from its immediate predecessors. Second, much of the cooperation that supported the system's key currencies was provided outside the IMF. This fact suggests that it was not the precise provisions of the Bretton Woods Agreement but rather its compatibility with ancillary arrangements negotiated by the industrial countries that lent the system its capacity to contain market pressures.

Also important for containing market pressures were capital controls. Controls were widely utilized throughout the Bretton Woods years; indeed until 1959 most industrial countries controlled foreign-exchange transactions on current as well as capital account.[23] Although controls could be circumvented eventually, doing so was costly, leaving governments some room for adjusting policy in stabilizing directions before the exchange rate collapsed or for arranging an orderly devaluation.

The literature on the decline and fall of the Bretton Woods System has traditionally emphasized its structural flaws.[24] Many of the arguments can be framed in terms of the concepts developed in chapter 3. The late 1960s saw a decline in the robustness of monetary policy in the United States, where monetary stability and defense of the $35 gold price were subordinated to the financial imperatives of the Vietnam War, and in Europe, where Euro-Keynesianism met with growing favor. Britain's stop-go policies, culminating in the 1967 sterling crisis, epitomized the tendency for macroeconomic policy-makers to vacillate in their pursuit of domestic and international economic objectives and to fail to adhere to a consistent policy line.

The decline in the robustness of monetary policy rules was followed by a predictable increase in the rigidity of the exchange rate system. Unable to appeal to a contingent rule, governments sought to buttress the credibility of their commitment to the exchange rate by resisting all pressures to devalue. Closing off the escape clause heightened the difficulty of adjusting relative prices. Once the escape clause was no longer available, other countries hesitated to cooperate in

23. Prominent exceptions were the United States, Canada, and a few Latin American countries. In Europe exchange rates were regulated under the aegis of the European Payments Union (EPU), which superimposed another layer of external monitors (the EPU Managing Board) and additional sources of external support (EPU credit lines) on top of the Bretton Woods System. Thus the success of the EPU is readily explicable in terms of the prerequisites for a viable international monetary system emphasized here. For details, see Triffin (1957); Eichengreen (1993b).

24. A comprehensive review of the literature on the collapse of the Bretton Woods System is provided by Garber (1993).

supporting currencies in distress for fear that they would incur massive financial obligations. International cooperation grew increasingly difficult with French President Charles de Gaulle's criticisms of the United States' "exorbitant privilege" and worries about the stability of the dollar.[25] Meanwhile, the growing porousness of capital controls weakened the defenses countries erected unilaterally to contain market pressures.[26] The collapse of the Bretton Woods System of pegged but adjustable exchange rates in 1971 was a predictable consequence.

Post–Bretton Woods Arrangements

The only generalization about post–Bretton Woods international monetary arrangements that can be advanced with confidence is that they resist generalization. Often called the post–Bretton Woods "nonsystem," international monetary arrangements over the last two decades have oscillated between unilateral efforts at exchange rate stabilization and ad hoc attempts at collaborative exchange rate management.

Three post–Bretton Woods initiatives are worth considering for the light they shed on the prerequisites for international monetary stability. The first is the unsuccessful attempt at exchange rate stabilization undertaken by European countries in the years during which the Bretton Woods System drew its final breaths. In 1972 the members of the European Economic Community established the "snake in the tunnel," whereby intra-European exchange rates were held within narrower margins than required by the Smithsonian Agreement. They created a Very Short-Term Financing Facility to help member countries bridge temporary balance-of-payments deficits.

Following the collapse of the Smithsonian "tunnel" in 1973, the snake was maintained but less than wholly successfully. Some countries left the system temporarily, others permanently. Only Germany and its small northern European neighbors adhered faithfully to the system. Gros and Thygesen emphasize two explanations for the failure of this initiative. One is overly expansionary monetary and fiscal

25. From this perspective, the dissolution of the gold pool in 1968 comes as no surprise.

26. Obstfeld (1993) analyzes changes over time in deviations from covered interest parity, a standard measure of the extent of capital controls and related barriers to international capital market integration. He concludes that "the results on the whole support the interpretation of the Bretton Woods period as one in which capital mobility was still imperfect, but increasing."

policies. The quadrupling of oil prices in the final quarter of 1973 and the recessions that followed induced governments to adopt counter-cyclical policies with inflationary consequences. By early 1976, inflation in Italy and the United Kingdom had accelerated to more than 20 percent and long since driven both countries out of the snake. Inflation rates were one-third to one-half lower in the most inflationary countries of the snake and significantly lower still in the anchor country, Germany. In 1975, in response to a deepening recession, France embarked on more expansionary fiscal policies, driving the franc out of the snake for a second time. Gros and Thygesen also blame inadequate coordination of policies across countries, caused by the unwillingness of governments to compromise domestic economic objectives or to delegate adequate authority to the Committee of Central Bank Governors and the European Monetary Cooperation Fund. In the language of chapter 3, the commitment to robust monetary rules was inadequate, and international cooperation did not suffice to contain market pressures.[27]

A second notable post–Bretton Woods initiative was the Plaza-Louvre accords initialed by finance ministers of the G-5 countries in the mid-1980s. The three major industrial-country currencies—the dollar, the deutsche mark, and the yen—had been left to float against one another in the first half of the 1980s. Between mid-1980 and mid-1985 the trade-weighted value of the dollar against foreign currencies had risen by nearly 90 percent, and the U.S. real exchange rate moved strongly in the same direction, eliciting protectionist pressures in the U.S. Congress. At the Plaza Hotel in New York in September 1985 the G-5 countries therefore agreed to adjust their monetary and fiscal policies with the aim of depreciating the dollar. By February 1987, having concluded that dollar depreciation had gone far enough, they negotiated at the Louvre an exchange rate stabilization agreement, described in chapter 2, which was designed to hold currencies within narrow bands.

Official purchases of dollars were far larger in the months following the Louvre Accord than at any other time following the collapse of the Bretton Woods System. Depreciation of the dollar was stemmed temporarily, and the dollar was held within its 2.5 percent band. But the accord was supported by neither the overriding commitment to

27. See Gros and Thygesen (1992).

exchange rate targeting nor the effective international cooperation needed for the smooth functioning of an agreement to stabilize exchange rates. The United States took no steps to address the yawning current account deficit that was undermining confidence in the dollar. In October 1987 the Bundesbank increased a key interest rate in response to a mild indication of domestic inflation, a step that raised new questions about whether its commitment to dollar stabilization was any stronger than that of the United States; the Reagan Administration was quick to criticize the German central bank. The U.S. stock market crashed the following Monday, leading the Fed to reduce interest rates and make credit available to the market irrespective of the implications for the exchange rate. Germany and Japan refused to support the dollar further unless the United States took steps to reduce its budget deficit. Thus both inadequate international cooperation and hesitation to pursue robust monetary rules attaching a priority to exchange rate stability led to the demise of the Louvre Accord.

The only initiative that might be held out as a serious step toward sustainable international monetary reform is the European Monetary System (EMS). Established in 1979 out of the remains of the snake, the EMS has evolved into an increasingly cohesive and ambitious exchange rate arrangement. Until the September 1992 crisis, the EMS was widely touted as a success. It was believed that it pointed the way toward international monetary reform on a global scale.

The prerequisites for a viable international monetary system emphasized in this study shed light on both the success of the EMS in the 1980s and its subsequent difficulties. The EMS by design made provision for accommodating disturbances and containing market pressures. Currencies were allowed to vary within a fluctuation band (normally 2.25 percent, but 6 percent in the case of the wider band temporarily accorded some new entrants to the system). Countries were permitted to alter their central parity in the event of persistent balance-of-payments disequilibria. From the inception of the EMS through January 1987 there were eleven realignments, on average more than one a year (see table 4-1).

However, the statement that governments resorted to realignment only in the event of shocks not of their own making is a dubious proposition. Most participating countries hardly followed what can be characterized as robust monetary rules; typically realignment was

Table 4-1. *Exchange Rate Realignments within the EMS, 1979–87*[a]

Date	Deutsche mark	Dutch guilder	French franc	Belgian-Luxembourg franc	Italian lira	Danish kroner	Irish punt
September 24, 1979	2.0	...	...	...	...	−2.9	...
November 30, 1979	...	...	...	...	...	−4.8	...
March 23, 1981	...	...	...	...	−6.0	...	...
October 5, 1981	5.5	5.5	−3.0	...	−3.0	...	...
February 22, 1982	...	...	...	−8.5	...	−3.0	...
June 14, 1982	4.25	4.25	−5.75	...	−2.75	...	...
March 21, 1983	5.5	3.5	−2.5	1.5	−2.5	2.5	−3.5
July 22, 1985	2.0	2.0	2.0	2.0	−6.0	2.0	2.0
April 7, 1986	3.0	3.0	−3.0	1.0	...	1.0	...
August 4, 1986	...	...	...	...	...	...	−8.0
January 12, 1987	3.0	3.0	...	2.0	...	...	...

Source: Fratianni and von Hagen (1992), p. 22.

a. The numbers are percentage changes of a given currency's bilateral central rate against those currencies whose bilateral parities were not realigned. A positive number denotes an appreciation, a negative number, a depreciation. On March 21, 1983, and on July 22, 1985, all parities were realigned.

provoked not by exogenous shocks but by persistent domestic inflation. The standard deviation of inflation rates across EMS countries actually rose in the first four years of the EMS compared to the preceding period (table 4-2). Nonetheless, the EMS requirement that a government wishing to change its parity first obtain the agreement of all other participating countries prevented significant abuses of the system.

That the EMS not only survived but prospered in the face of less than robust monetary policies is a tribute to the devices used to contain market pressures. Prominent among these was the Very Short-Term Financing Facility, permitting weak-currency countries to borrow from their stronger counterparts to defend their exchange rates.[28] Short-term financing was increased from 6 to 14 billion ECU, and medium-term financing ceilings were raised from 5.45 to 14.1 billion ECU. According to the EMS Act of Foundation, when a bilateral exchange rate reached the maximum permissible distance from its central parity, both central banks concerned were required to intervene. The Basle-Nyborg Agreement of 1987 made allowance for intramarginal interventions.

What political conditions lent credibility to strong-currency countries' promise to support their weak-currency counterparts? One

28. This facility had actually been established in conjunction with the snake, as described previously.

Table 4-2. *Average Annual Inflation Rates in Europe, 1974–89*[a]

Rates in percent with standard deviations in parentheses

Item	1974–78	1979–82	1983–86	1987–89
Average EMS	9.9 (3.6)	10.4 (4.4)	4.6 (2.3)	2.3 (1.1)
Average EC non-EMS	16.3 (3.5)	16.1 (3.6)	12.6 (5.9)	6.6 (2.5)
Average Europe non-EC	8.4 (3.5)	8.8 (2.0)	5.2 (1.8)	3.7 (0.9)

Source: Gros and Thygesen (1992), p. 112.

a. Europe non-EC includes Switzerland, Norway, Sweden, and Finland.

answer, explored in chapter 7, is that strong-currency countries agreed to extend support because their weak-currency counterparts promised to resort to the escape clause, realigning their currencies downward, when fundamentals diverged from those consistent with the existing parity; this commitment to realign limited the strong-currency countries' obligations sufficiently to elicit their willing support.[29] Another answer, also pursued subsequently, is that the EMS was linked to other European Community agreements providing implicit compensation to the countries extending support.

A conspicuous feature of the EMS was the maintenance of capital controls. These took a variety of forms, ranging from taxes on holdings of foreign-currency assets to restrictions on the ability of banks to lend abroad. Along with realignments and the Very Short-Term Financing Facility, controls squared the circle. The knowledge that weak-currency countries would ultimately realign reassured their strong-currency counterparts that intervention obligations were limited. Capital controls, though porous, provided sufficient insulation to arrange orderly realignments before governments were overwhelmed by speculative pressures, thus ensuring the survival of the system.

The changing balance among these elements in the period leading up to the September 1992 EMS crisis sheds light on which ones were essential to the system's operation. Adherence to robust monetary rules, though still far from perfect, grew more rather than less prevalent as the period progressed (for evidence, see table 4-2). What grew less prevalent was resort to the escape clause. From February 1987 until the September 1992 crisis, no realignments took place. This shift was a corollary of the removal of capital controls, which were a casualty of the Single European Act designed to create an integrated

29. This was the German Bundesbank's understanding. See the discussion in chapter 5.

European market.[30] The removal of controls made orderly realignments more difficult to arrange. Countries consequently attempted to pursue policies obviating the need to realign. With the increasing rigidity of the exchange rate system, strong-currency countries like Germany lost confidence that realignment by weak-currency countries would limit intervention obligations to acceptable levels; unlimited intervention threatened price stability, something that countries like Germany were unwilling to countenance. Thus just as balance-of-payments pressures were building, the EMS's traditional means of containing them were being weakened or removed. German economic and monetary union, as an asymmetric shock undermining the competitiveness of Germany's partners in the European Monetary System, further exacerbated these problems. The events of 1992 thus culminated in a crisis that drove two currencies from the Exchange Rate Mechanism and weakened confidence in others. A second speculative crisis less than a year later forced the virtual dismantling of the EMS.

Summary

This analysis of recent EMS history illustrates a general proposition: increases in capital mobility make international monetary arrangements based on exchange rate targets—pegged but adjustable rates, target zones, and the like—increasingly difficult to operate. International capital flows have already reached very high levels. Insofar as further increases are inevitable, governments may be confronted with a stark choice: to abandon explicit exchange rate targets or contemplate monetary unification. The next chapter develops this point.

30. The act had mandated their elimination by July 1, 1990, except in Spain and Ireland, which were exempted until December 31, 1992, and Portugal and Greece, which were exempted until December 31, 1995. In addition, the act allowed for emergency controls for a period of no more than six months. The Maastricht Treaty, however, rules out their use for any period from the beginning of Stage II on January 1, 1994.

Chapter 5

The Challenge of Deep Integration

COUNTRIES have traditionally been able to select from a menu of international monetary arrangements arrayed along the spectrum from freely floating to all but permanently fixed exchange rates. Most have preferred policies framed in terms of contingent exchange rate targets combining elements of the two extremes. The thesis of this chapter is that policy rules entailing contingent exchange rate targets will no longer be viable in the twenty-first century.

Mounting Market Pressures

Defense of an exchange rate peg or target requires that governments be able to resist market pressures. They must be able to rebuff the kind of speculative attacks, described in chapter 3, that are not grounded in fundamentals. The capital mobility characteristic of the late twentieth century makes such resistance extremely costly and potentially unsustainable politically.

The proximate source of the problem is the magnitude of the resources that can be brought to bear against a currency peg. Total cross-border ownership of tradable securities has risen to an estimated $2.5 trillion as of 1992. Most of these assets are highly liquid. The foreign exchange market is now the world's largest financial market. Net daily turnover in nine of the major national markets is estimated to approach $1 trillion (see table 5-1).[1] This is a new development: the

---

1. Certain segments of the market, notably swaps, outright forwards, and options, have grown significantly faster than these averages.

Table 5-1. *Global Foreign Exchange Market Turnover, Corrected for Double-Counting and Estimated Gaps in Reporting, 1989–92*
Daily averages, in billions of U.S. dollars

Source of turnover	April 1989[a]	April 1992[b]		Percent change[c]
Total reported gross turnover	932	1,354	(1,263)	35
With other reporting local banks and dealers	377	447	(428)	[14]
Spot transactions, outright forward, and swaps	. . .	433	(415)	. . .
OTC options[d]	. . .	14	(14)	
With banks and dealers located abroad	431	630	(570)	[32]
Spot transactions, outright forward, and swaps	. . .	615	(555)	. . .
OTC options[d]	. . .	15	(15)	
All other[d]	124	277	(264)	n.a.
Adjustment for domestic double-counting[e]	−189	−223	(−214)	. . .
Spot transactions, outright forward, and swaps	. . .	−217	(−207)	. . .
OTC options	. . .	−7	(−7)	
Total reported turnover net of local double-counting ("net gross")	744	1,130	(1,048)	41
Adjustment for cross-border double-counting[a,e]	−184	−298	(−270)	. . .
Total reported "net-net" turnover	560	832	(778)	39
Estimated gaps in reporting[a]	60	48	102	. . .
Estimated global turnover[e]	620	880	880	42
All "traditional" market segments[f]	590	820	820	39
Spot transactions	350	400	400	15
Options and futures	30	60	60	100

Source: Group of Ten (1993, p. 117).

n.a. Not available.

a. Changes have been made to the earlier published estimates of both cross-border double-counting and gaps in reporting in 1989.

b. Figures in parentheses relate to countries providing data in both 1989 and 1992. Within these countries, coverage became slightly more comprehensive.

c. Except for estimated global turnover, percent changes are calculated using data from countries reporting data in both years but, owing to changes in the classification of counterparties, the figures in square brackets are only indicative.

d. Estimates based on the assumption that one-half of the over-the-counter (OTC) options business with nondealer counterparties ($16 billion) and the gross options business conducted via organized exchanges ($5 billion) is included in "all other." This category also includes gross turnover in futures ($9 billion) as well as other business with nondealer counterparties. In 1989 this category contained all estimated (non-interbank) business with "customers."

e. No adjustment was made for double-counting of exchange-traded options and futures or for countries not providing counterparty information on OTC options transactions. On the assumption that all such business was with other reporting entities the maximum double-counting in 1992 would have been roughly $10 billion.

f. Spot, outright forward, and swap transactions.

Table 5-2. *Markets for Selected Derivative Instruments,*
Selected Years, 1986–91

Notional principal amounts outstanding at end of year, in billions of U.S. dollars
equivalent

Instrument	1986	1989	1990	1991
Exchange-traded instruments[a]	583	1,762	2,284	3,518
Interest rate futures	370	1,201	1,454	2,159
Interest rate options[b]	146	387	600	1,072
Currency futures	10	16	16	18
Currency options[b]	39	50	56	59
Stock market index futures	15	42	70	77
Options on stock market indexes[b]	3	66	88	132
Over-the-counter instruments[c]	500 (e)	2,402	3,451	4,449
Interest rate swaps[d]	400 (e)	1,503	2,312	3,065
Currency and cross-currency interest rate swaps[d,e]	100 (e)	449	578	807
Other derivative instruments[d,f]	...	450	561	577
Memorandum item: Cross-border plus local foreign currency claims of Bank for International Settlements reporting banks	4,031	6,498	7,578	7,497

Source: Bank for International Settlements (1992), cited in Group of Ten (1993, p. 95).

(e) = Estimate.

a. Excludes options on individual shares and derivatives involving commodity contracts.

b. Calls plus puts.

c. Excludes information on contracts such as forward rate agreements, over-the-counter currency options, forward exchange positions, equity swaps, and warrants on equity.

d. Contracts between ISDA members are reported only once.

e. Adjusted for reporting of both currencies.

f. Caps. dollar, floors, and swaptions.

volume of transactions more than quadrupled between 1986 and 1992.[2] That volume has been reported to rise dramatically—by a factor of two or three—in periods of intense speculation.[2]

These trends reflect financial innovation. Improvements in trading and settlement practices and advances in computer and communications technologies have enabled banks and other financial institutions to handle a larger volume of foreign exchange transactions at lower cost and with minimal risk of settlement failure. The development of derivative instruments such as futures and options (table 5-2) has enabled investors to unbundle risks, facilitating portfolio diversification. In addition, the growth in the volume of transactions reflects

2. Group of Ten (1993, p. 15).

positive steps by governments, notably their removal of capital controls. Countries like the United States and Japan have also abolished regulations limiting the share of institutional portfolios that may be held in foreign assets, stimulating cross-border diversification (table 5-3).[3] They have harmonized accounting standards and disclosure requirements, helping to disseminate information on the creditworthiness of international borrowers.

This is a specific instance of the deregulatory trend characteristic of economic policy in the 1980s and 1990s. To cite but one example, the Single European Act mandating the removal of capital controls by European Community (EC) member states was part of an effort to enhance economic efficiency by forging an integrated internal market unfettered by regulatory restraints.[4] The relaxation and removal of capital controls have not been limited to Europe, however; they are also evident in Japan, Latin America, and other parts of the world.[5] The pervasiveness of the phenomenon suggests that the removal of controls and other steps taken by governments to liberalize foreign exchange transactions reflect common pressures affecting all countries, namely the tendency for changes in technology and market structure to increase the costs of pursuing policies designed to segment capital markets. For example, discouraging purchases of foreign currency by requiring banks with open positions in foreign exchange to place non-interest-bearing deposits with their central banks was easier to do when all foreign exchange transactions passed through banks, when it was not possible to use derivative instruments to disguise open positions, and when banks did not possess offshore subsidiaries with which to book those transactions. With these innovations, discouraging purchases of foreign currency requires the establishment of an ever more extensive regulatory apparatus. In part, the decision to eliminate capital controls reflects the consequent increase in the cost of implementing such measures.[6]

3. For details, see Goldstein and others (1993); Group of Ten (1993).

4. This is not to deny that there existed a strand of thought that viewed the Single Market as a means of minimizing pressure for competitive deregulation and for harmonizing social and regulatory policies at a high level throughout the Community.

5. A comprehensive survey of capital account liberalization is Mathieson and Rojas-Suarez (1993).

6. A critical question, obviously, is whether these trends might be reversed. International capital mobility was also extensive under the classical gold standard, as described

Together these changes in technology, policy, and market structure have created an enormous pool of liquid funds ready to move at the first hint of devaluation risk. Foreign asset positions are actively managed by institutional investors like mutual and pension funds (table 5-4).[7] Fund managers in the business of monitoring current developments are able to alter the composition of their portfolios at low cost. Improvements in trading and information systems and back-office clearance and settlement systems have increased the speed and reduced the cost at which transactions can be undertaken. Already the volume of net daily foreign exchange transactions exceeds the total official reserves of all International Monetary Fund member countries combined. (These approached $750 billion in September 1992, the last episode of intense one-way speculation.) The otherwise impressive quantities of intervention in which the EC countries engaged during the 1992 European Monetary System (EMS) crisis— $46 billion in July and August, $228 billion in September and October—pale in comparison with the $20 trillion of foreign exchange transactions conducted each month.[8]

Implications for International Monetary Arrangements

The extent of the resources that the markets can bring to bear makes it difficult to hold out in the face of speculative pressures. This is especially true when systems of pegged but adjustable rates and narrow target zones offer one-way bets. If the zone is narrow, there is little scope for a weak exchange rate to appreciate, creating scant danger of capital losses. But if the peg is abandoned and the rate depreciates significantly, speculators stand to reap very substantial capital gains. The removal of capital controls and improvements in trading technologies reduce the costs of placing this one-way bet.

---

in chapter 4, yet that process was reversed in the interwar period largely as a result of government action. I argue in this chapter that changes in technology make another such reversal unlikely in the twenty-first century even if there is another marked swing in sentiment among policymakers. The same implication may be drawn from the arguments of Mussa and Goldstein (1994) and Crockett (1994).

7. This trend can be expected to persist: it has been estimated that the share of foreign assets in the portfolios of the world's three hundred largest pension funds, for example, will rise from 7 to 12 percent over the next five years; see Group of Ten (1993, p. 6).

8. See Alogoskoufis (1993). These figures refer to gross intervention.

Table 5-3. *Institutional Investors' Holdings of Foreign Securities,*
Selected Years, 1980–91
Percent of total securities holdings

Investor	1980[a]	1985[b]	1990	1991
United States				
Private pension funds[c]	1.0	3.0	4.2	5.2
Japan				
Life insurance companies	9.0	26.4	30.0	28.4
Non–life insurance companies	7.4	19.4	29.1	28.5
Trust accounts of banks	2.2	14.0	19.4	22.1
Postal life insurance	0.0	6.7	11.6	12.1
Norinchukin Bank	4.3	10.3	22.7	32.6
Canada				
Life insurance companies	2.1	2.2	2.3	2.7
Pension funds	6.1	6.6	6.0	7.6
Italy				
Insurance companies	11.7	10.1	11.6	9.7
United Kingdom[d]				
Insurance companies	6.9	17.3	20.7	. . .
Pension funds	10.3	17.8	23.6	. . .
Belgium				
Insurance companies and pension funds	1.7	3.3	3.3	. . .
Netherlands				
Insurance companies	5.2	10.3	9.3	10.3
Private pension funds	10.6	13.8	21.1	23.5
Public pension funds	1.7	2.8	5.2	5.7
Sweden				
Insurance companies	. . .	1.5	10.4	12.5

Source: Takeda and Turner (1992), cited in Group of Ten (1993, p. 92).

a. For the Netherlands, 1983 figures.

b. For Sweden, 1987 figures.

c. Tax-exempt funded schemes (excluding IRAs).

d. Pension funds exclude central government sector but include other public sectors. Unit trust investment allocated as follows: 50 percent foreign and 50 percent at end of 1989 (on the basis of partial survey results); other years calculated in proportion to changes in the measured share of foreign assets.

Table 5-4. *The Growth of Institutional Investors, 1980–90*
Financial assets as percent of household financial assets

Country	Pension funds and life insurance companies			Collective investment institutions			Total		
	1980	1985	1990[a]	1980	1985	1990[a]	1980	1985	1990[a]
United States	17.8	21.1	23.5	2.2	5.0	7.7	20.0	26.0	31.2
Japan	13.8	16.6	20.8	1.8	3.6	5.6	15.6	20.2	26.4
Germany	19.4	24.4	27.1	3.2	4.8	8.1	22.6	29.0	35.1
France	8.0	11.2	14.7	2.7	12.4	21.7	10.6	23.6	36.3
Italy[b,c]	1.6	0.9	3.2	n.a.	2.1	2.9	n.a.	2.9	6.1
United Kingdom[b]	39.9	49.9	53.7	1.6	3.1	4.9	41.5	53.1	58.6
Canada	19.4	23.3	26.7	1.0	1.6	3.0	20.4	24.9	29.7

Source: Group of Ten (1993, p. 89).
n.a. Not available.
a. For Italy and United Kingdom, 1989 figures.
b. Total assets.
c. At book value.

There is no better authority on this point than the currency speculator George Soros (writing before the famous episode of speculation against the Bank of England in which he participated in the summer of 1992):

> Target zones are unlikely to discourage speculation. On the contrary, they may constitute an invitation to speculate against the authorities with limited risk. By endorsing a set of target zones, the authorities would expose themselves to speculative attack at a time and place to be chosen by the speculators. History shows that under these conditions the speculators usually win.[9]

It is hard to imagine a clearer description of the problem.

With the rise in international financial transactions, the supply of speculative capital that can be brought to bear against a currency whose stability is placed in doubt is in effect perfectly elastic. Chapter 3 identified three techniques for containing these pressures: increased interest rates, capital controls, and unlimited foreign support. What are the implications of deep financial integration for the effectiveness of each?

Reimposition of Capital Controls

The four decades before 1913 were a period of rising international capital mobility much like the late twentieth century. With the laying

9. Soros (1987, p. 328).

of the transatlantic cable and other improvements in communication and transportation, arbitrage in international financial markets was enhanced. Capital flows reached high levels.[10] Yet this trend was reversed in the 1930s by the reimposition of capital controls. Could a similar reversal effectively suppress the rise of international capital mobility?

There are two reasons to believe that the answer is no. First, improvements in trading practices and advances in transaction technologies make capital controls increasingly difficult to enforce. Computer technologies allow capital to move internationally at the flick of a key. Derivative instruments allow it to be repackaged in a myriad of forms. The growing interpenetration of direct foreign investments makes it easier to use foreign subsidiaries to manipulate transfer prices to circumvent exchange restrictions. Enforcing controls will therefore require an increasingly onerous regulatory apparatus. Administering them will become prohibitively costly and disruptive of other commercial and financial activities. Changes in technology and market structure will therefore continue to militate against their use.

The same problems existed in the 1930s, of course, but to a lesser extent. The range of financial instruments and intermediaries being more limited, controls were simpler to enforce. The fact that it was possible in the past to limit international financial transactions at an acceptable cost does not mean that the same will be possible in the future.[11]

Second, applying capital controls at a tolerable cost will require coordination among countries. Controls imposed unilaterally by one country are capable of creating a wedge between onshore and offshore interest rates and reducing the impact on the domestic economy of the policies needed to defend the exchange rate, but only at the cost of sacrificing domestic financial activity. Currency trading and other financial transactions will move offshore, dealing

---

10. For details and estimates, see Bloomfield (1963) and Bayoumi (1990).

11. Some readers may find this view surprising coming from an author who has, in the European context, proposed the imposition of a temporary transactions tax on foreign exchange dealing or the application of non-interest-bearing deposit requirements on banks with open foreign exchange positions; see Eichengreen and Wyplosz (1993). The difference is that those measures were proposed as temporary expedients to remain in force only until the European countries in question completed their transition to monetary union. In addition, for all the reasons detailed in the text, a proposal that is attractive now may be less so in a future with even more articulated international financial markets.

a blow to efforts to encourage the development of domestic financial markets.[12] The solution to this problem is for countries to agree to the simultaneous application of controls. The obstacle is the free-rider problem: the temptation for a country to refuse to cooperate in the hope that it will capture the financial business fleeing other centers.

Why was this less of a problem in the past? In part there was less financial business to lose. A smaller share of claims on enterprises were traded in the form of liquid securities. There existed fewer competing financial centers, limiting the options available to investors and rendering the free-rider problem easier to solve. A more restrictive range of financial assets and intermediaries limited the opportunities for moving financial business offshore. Thus even if the implications of unilaterally imposed controls for the competitiveness of domestic financial markets were not prohibitive in the past, they may be in the future.

Increased Interest Rates

In principle a central bank can raise interest rates to whatever heights are required to render investors indifferent to the choice between holding domestic and foreign assets, thereby sustaining an exchange rate peg. Deep integration increases the costs of applying this instrument, however, possibly to politically intolerable heights.

Interest rate increases will be particularly costly for countries with high levels of public debt. If domestic and foreign government bonds are close substitutes, as tends to be the case when financial markets are integrated, expectations of an impending devaluation will cause a wholesale shift out of domestic bonds unless investors are compensated by a commensurate increase in domestic interest rates.[13] If taxation is highly distortionary, raising the additional revenues needed to pay the debt service costs associated with increased interest rates will be especially painful. Thus interest rate increases may widen

12. This was Spain's experience when it temporarily reimposed controls in the second half of 1992.

13. When domestic and foreign government bonds are imperfect substitutes and international financial markets are imperfectly integrated, the requisite increase in interest rates will be moderated. In fact, however, the empirical evidence, cited in chapter 2, suggests that the risk premiums that would result from imperfect substitutability are small to the extent that they exist at all.

the budget deficit, worsening the currency crisis rather than resolving it. Deep integration may thereby limit a government's ability to employ the interest rate defense.

Worse still, deep integration may induce self-fulfilling balance-of-payments crises for countries in this position. The increase in taxation needed to finance the extra debt service may be so costly and distortionary that the government will be unable to undertake it.[14] Currency traders will have reason to anticipate that the authorities will be forced to abandon their policies of monetary stringency and monetize the resulting deficit. Even if, in the absence of an attack, monetary and fiscal policies are consistent with indefinite maintenance of the currency peg, a speculative crisis that forces an increase in the level of interest rates may prove self-fulfilling.[15]

Moreover, in an environment in which investors can choose between domestic and foreign bonds, fears of devaluation induced by the rise in interest rates may lead them to hesitate to roll over their maturing treasury securities, and the government may find itself in a funding crisis in which the central bank is forced to buy up the maturing debt irrespective of the inflationary consequences.[16] If further increases in taxes are prohibitively costly, the government may have to resort to inflationary finance. Once again even if underlying policies are seemingly consistent with maintenance of the exchange rate peg, the funding crisis induced by the attack may nonetheless render the latter self-fulfilling.

Another circumstance in which interest rate increases can be so costly as to prompt a government confronted with a speculative crisis to abandon its currency peg is when the condition of the banking system is weak.[17] Increases in central bank interest rates are passed

14. A model of self-fulfilling balance-of-payments crises when interest rate increases raise the burden of servicing the public debt is provided by Obstfeld (1994). The model assumes an optimizing government that may hesitate to raise taxes to support a currency peg when the social cost of further tax increases is high.

15. The realism of these fears is illustrated by the case of Italy, where the debt-to-income ratio exceeds unity and every percentage point increase in interest rates adds significantly to the budget deficit. Of the Italian government's debt, 29 percent takes the form of treasury bills and 48 percent is in the form of floating rate securities. Together these amount to some 84 per cent of gross domestic production (GDP). Raising interest rates by a point for one year therefore increases the budget deficit by about a percentage point of GDP. See Eichengreen and Wyplosz (1993, p. 104).

16. For models of funding crises, see Alesina, Prati, and Tabellini (1990); Giavazzi and Pagano (1990).

17. Obstfeld (1994) discusses this case as well.

through into interbank rates, raising costs for banks requiring overnight funding of their balance sheets.[18] These increases tend to aggravate the problem of nonperforming assets on bank balance sheets. Where the condition of the banking system is already weak, dramatic interest rate increases can raise the specter of bank failures. Investors may have good reason to anticipate that high interest rates that provoke loan defaults will so weaken the banks that the government will hesitate to defend its currency peg at the expense of destabilizing the banking system.

Note again that the consequent balance-of-payments crisis can be self-fulfilling. In the absence of an attack, the banking system may have only modest problems, monetary and fiscal policies may be in balance, and the exchange rate peg may be sustainable indefinitely. But if an attack occurs, the induced instability of the banking system may raise the costs of defending the exchange rate peg to unsustainable heights, forcing its abandonment.

A third circumstance in which the interest rate defense can be ineffectual is when increased rates produce an intolerable rise in unemployment. If the perceived social costs of unemployment rise with its level, policies that further aggravate unemployment may prove impossible to bear when its level is already high. It may be impossible to counter a speculative attack with an increase in interest rates that depresses aggregate demand still further. Even if the central bank chooses to raise interest rates, doing so may augur a predictable political backlash that will force a subsequent interest rate reduction. Since speculators are forward looking, the initial increase will not deter them from betting against the currency. Under these circumstances, the initial interest rate increase will be ineffectual, and the speculative attack can be self-fulfilling.[19]

Foreign Support

The only remaining defense against speculative attacks in a world of high capital mobility is foreign support. Foreign governments and central banks can replenish the international reserves of

18. The experience of Sweden in September 1992 illustrates the point; see Goldstein and others (1993, p. 56).

19. This kind of situation is modeled formally by Ozkan and Sutherland (1994).

the country under attack. They can purchase its currency on the open market.

In principle, there are no limits to the effectiveness of this defense. Foreign central banks and governments can purchase however many units of foreign exchange are sold by traders. In practice, however, extensive foreign support may have adverse consequences for the countries extending it, which will limit their willingness to offer it.

The obvious consequence is inflation. The strong-currency country will have to purchase all the assets of the weak-currency country that speculators wish to sell. In a world where purchasing power parity is even a rough guide to the long-run equilibrium value of an exchange rate, supporting the currency of a high-inflation country may require bringing inflation in other countries up to the level prevailing in the country under attack.[20] If the strong-currency countries could be certain that specific policy adaptations in the weak-currency countries would follow, they might be willing to extend however much support was required to preserve the currency peg. If inflationary tendencies in the weak-currency countries were reined in, foreign support could be provided without a danger of significant inflationary consequences for the creditor country.

In a world of sovereign governments, however, there can be no certainty that the requisite policy adjustments will follow. Therefore, foreign support is necessarily limited. Strong-currency countries will no more be willing to extend unlimited support to their weak-currency counterparts than would a commercial bank be willing to extend unlimited credit unconditionally to a private borrower.[21]

This observation explains what would otherwise be paradoxical features of various international monetary arrangements. The Act of Foundation of the EMS, for example, provides explicitly for foreign support.[22] It speaks of "unlimited" interventions at "compulsory"

20. This follows directly if the only form of intervention capable of affecting exchange rates is unsterilized. Even if intervention is partially sterilized, as in the case of Bundesbank intervention in support of other EMS currencies in September 1992, it may be taken to signal a greater future willingness to relax the commitment to price stability in order to defend foreign currencies, as discussed in chapter 2.

21. An interesting exception is the countries using "francs des Colonies Françaises d'Afrique" (CFA francs), which compromise their sovereignty by giving seats on their central bank boards to the former colonial power. Consistent with the present argument, France extends essentially unlimited support in return. For details see chapter 8.

22. The discussion here draws on Vaubel (1980); Begg and Wyplosz (1993); Eichengreen and Wyplosz (1993).

intervention rates. It requires participating central banks to open for one another Very Short-Term Credit Facilities "unlimited in amount." Yet the history of the EMS clearly demonstrates that intervention is not unlimited. In September 1992, for example, there was no technical obstacle to the Bundesbank purchasing British pounds and Italian lire in whatever quantities were required to prevent sterling and the lira from depreciating against the deutsche mark. But while the Bundesbank fulfilled its technical obligations, it also made clear to its EMS partners that it hesitated to continue doing so indefinitely.[23] Fear of the inflationary consequences is the obvious explanation. Over the weekend preceding Italy's devaluation Bundesbank President Helmut Schlesinger reportedly sought to arrange a general realignment of EMS currencies.[24] Had the other currencies been devalued against the deutsche mark, the Bundesbank's intervention obligations would have been limited, and the link between inflation in Germany and elsewhere in the EMS would have been broken. For reasons that remain unclear, however, a realignment proved impossible to arrange.

In justifying its actions, the Bundesbank could appeal to an agreement with the German government, which dated from the time the EMS was established. This stated that the Ministry of Finance would not hold the Bundesbank to its unlimited intervention obligation if doing so threatened the central bank's commitment to price stability. If it could not be reassured that other countries would take corrective measures to stem their inflation and balance-of-payments deficits, then the Bundesbank would be relieved of its intervention obligation.[25]

Much space has been devoted to this episode in order to make a general point, namely the unrealism of anticipating unlimited foreign support for currencies in distress. Unlimited intervention can have unlimited costs and will not be extended unless binding conditions

23. It is not clear from the evidence that has been made available to date whether the Bundesbank ever told its EMS partners explicitly that they could not expect further support. But many sources (cited in chapter 7) point to the conclusion that other EMS countries had good reason to anticipate that the Bundesbank would do so eventually.

24. For details see Eichengreen and Wyplosz (1993).

25. This understanding between the Finance Ministry and the Bundesbank is described in the memoirs of the then-president of the central bank, Otmar Emminger (1986, pp. 361–62). Whether a decision to invoke this agreement would have placed the Bundesbank in technical violation of its EMS agreements with other EC central banks is academic, since other currencies were realigned before the provision was actually invoked. The same was true in the July 1993 episode.

are attached. And when applied to a sovereign nation, the necessary conditions are ultimately unenforceable.

Implications for Two Proposals for International Monetary Reform

Two popular proposals for international monetary reform that involve explicit exchange rate targets are Hanke, Jonung, and Schuler's proposal for currency boards and Williamson's blueprint for target zones. This section explores the implications of the preceding analysis for the viability of these options, since they might be thought to be less susceptible than other exchange-rate-targeting schemes to the forces eroding the viability of exchange rate targets.

Currency Boards

The attraction of a currency board is that it is expressly designed to minimize uncertainty about the authorities' commitment to defending their exchange rate peg. Statute prohibits the monetary authorities from issuing currency except when they acquire foreign exchange reserves adequate to convert that currency at a fixed rate. For every dollar's worth of domestic currency they issue, for example, they must possess a dollar's worth of reserves. Under such a system, the credibility of the pegged rate of exchange should be complete. Since speculators have no incentive to test the resolve of the monetary authorities, speculative attacks should be absent.

A recent example of this kind of arrangement is the Estonian currency board.[26] Under a law passed by the Estonian Parliament in May 1992, the currency (the kroon) must be fully backed by foreign exchange. The Bank of Estonia can alter the quantity of notes and coin in circulation only by acquiring additional foreign reserves. The Bank stands ready to convert kroons into deutsche marks for most current account transactions. The exchange rate is pegged to the deutsche mark at the rate of 1 DM = 8 EEK, with allowable fluctuations of plus or minus 3 percent. The Bank is divided into issue and banking departments, the first of which runs the currency board while

26. See Hanke, Jonung, and Schuler (1992).

the second is responsible for other central banking functions, including oversight of the payments and commercial banking systems.

Is this a truly fixed and unadjustable exchange rate? The Bank of Estonia is independent of the government, yet nothing prevents the parliament from changing the relevant law. Though the central bank currently has no discretion over the level of the peg beyond the 6 percent band, there remains the possibility that the currency law will someday be changed. It could be revoked or modified by the parliament in response to changing economic or political conditions. Lainela and Sutela argue that Estonian officials in fact understand their currency board to be a transitional arrangement to be abandoned in the not-too-distant future.[27] For speculators, solving backward, this raises questions about the credibility of the current peg.

That past performance provides no ironclad future guarantee is evidenced by the experience of Ireland. The Irish pound was unalterably fixed to the British pound sterling for more than 150 years, but even that exceptionally durable link was broken in 1979. As Portes puts the point, "'Permanently fixed exchange rates' is an oxymoron."[28] The exchange rate only exists so that it might one day be changed.[29]

The implication is that a currency board statute provides less than complete insulation against speculative attacks. Requiring an act of parliament before the exchange rate peg can be abandoned would presumably compel the Bank of Estonia, in the event of an attack, to maintain the interest rate defense for a longer period, irrespective of the domestic consequences of high interest rates, than if it possessed the authority to abandon the peg unilaterally. But the political fallout from high interest rates would be felt by the parliament rather than the central bank. Though significant political costs might be incurred when revising the statute prohibiting changes in the exchange rate, nothing else would insulate the parliament from pressures to do so. The knowledge that there might come a point at which it had the incentive to change the currency board statute could still provide speculators with the incentive to mount an attack.

27. See Lainela and Sutela (1993).
28. Portes (1993, p. 2). Compare Gandolfo (1992, p. 768): "The expression 'irrevocably fixed exchange rates' has no practical significance. . . . History is full of irrevocable commitments to fixed exchange rates that have broken down."
29. This has been the view of most academic analysts in the wake of the 1992 EMS crisis; see, for example, De Grauwe (1993).

Given the political costs of changing an act of parliament, an exchange rate fixed by a currency board statute should be more resilient than alternative arrangements in the face of a speculative crisis; speculators, knowing this, are less likely to mount an attack. But the fact remains that currency board statutes are readily changed, leaving scope for self-fulfilling attacks.

Target Zones

In Williamson's original proposal for a target zone system for the industrial countries, participants would preannounce bands for their real effective exchange rates, specifying a central rate surrounded by a 10 percent margin on either side.[30] Governments would manage their nominal exchange rates using foreign exchange market intervention and monetary policy so as to keep them in the band. Periodic realignments, to be undertaken before the edges of the band were reached, would avert the danger of speculative attacks. In this respect, the arrangement would resemble a system of crawling pegs (surrounded by bands), in which the rate of crawl would be governed by relative national rates of inflation. In addition, the system would feature "soft buffers," which would allow the rate to move outside the band under exceptional circumstances.

In thinking about the performance characteristics of such a system, it is worth noting both its similarities to and differences from the EMS, since that arrangement proved so problematic in the early 1990s. The EMS specified central rates and bands for each participating currency vis-à-vis baskets of other European currencies. It allowed intervention by governments and central banks to keep currencies within their bands and mandated intervention when the edge of the band was reached. It allowed for periodic realignments of the central rate.

The Williamson proposal differs from the EMS in the width of its bands (wider than the 2.25 percent bands of the pre-1993 EMS, narrower than the 15 percent bands of the subsequent system). It differs in *requiring* the bands to be shifted before their edges are

---

30. Williamson (1985). The proposal is generalized in Williamson and Miller (1987). Williamson and Miller propose negotiating current account targets and selecting central rates designed to hit them; I leave aside this aspect of their "blueprint."

reached if the weakness of an exchange rate reflects an underlying competitiveness problem. It allows commitments to intervene to be suspended when that weakness reflects speculation not prompted by underlying competitive difficulties.

Many of these features are attractive. The provision requiring the bands to be shifted before their edges are reached would prevent a build-up of competitiveness problems when the bottom of the band was approached from offering speculators a one-way bet and prompting them to attack. The soft buffer provision allowing the band to be temporarily disregarded in the event of an attack not prompted by fundamentals would allow the authorities to let the rate depreciate rather than raise domestic interest rates, ensuring the survival of the system. Once it became clear to speculators that the authorities were not inclined to alter the policies governing the evolution of fundamentals in response to the attack, the exchange rate should recover and move back into the band.

As noted in chapter 2, the advantage of target zones is the "bias in the band," the fact that a credible commitment to defense of a target zone will reduce the amount of exchange rate variability associated with given fundamentals, creating a "target zone honeymoon." Less monetary policy intervention will therefore be needed to stabilize the rate. Hence the trade-off between exchange rate stability and domestic monetary policy autonomy will be relaxed.

Will the Williamson proposal create a target zone honeymoon? If bands are shifted as soon as a differential develops between domestic and foreign interest rates, there is no reason for the markets to anticipate that the band will be defended, and there will be no bias in the band. On the contrary, this is precisely the circumstance in which the target zone honeymoon may give way to Bertola and Caballero's target zone divorce: an acceleration in inflation that increases expectations of realignment can increase the exchange rate volatility associated with given fundamentals within the band.[31] A more complicated set of monetary policy intervention rules might give rise to more complex fluctuations, but the resulting exchange rate behavior would

---

31. Bertola and Caballero (1990). Here *an acceleration in inflation* is used as shorthand for any development that would undermine the international competitiveness of a country. Soft buffers, which allow the edges of the band to be breached even in the absence of an acceleration in inflation, may provide motivation for speculators to mount an attack even when there is no inflationary event to prompt them.

not be obviously superior to that which would result from the kind of managed floating that would exist in the absence of target zones.

If, on the other hand, policymakers resist pressures to shift the band, allowing its boundaries to be reached and then intervening to prevent the rate from moving further, they expose themselves to the kind of crises that upset the narrow-band EMS in 1993. In order to produce the bias in the band, they will have to raise interest rates to defend the band's edges. In an environment of virtually unlimited market liquidity and no capital controls, the requisite interest rate increases, as in Europe in the summer of 1993, may prove infeasible.[32] Defending the band may only produce crises and no target zone honeymoon.

Thus "permissive" target zones in which bands are shifted before they are tested or in which soft buffers are repeatedly invoked would not differ significantly from managed floating, whereas a "robust" target zone in which the edges of the band are defended would not differ significantly from systems of pegged but adjustable rates whose viability has already been undermined by the integration of the world economy and the rise of capital mobility.

What Options Remain?

Ongoing changes in the world economy will undermine the viability of arrangements designed to prevent the exchange rate from exceeding explicit limits. Doubts about the credibility of policymakers' commitment to the defense of such limits, which are inevitable in a democracy, will prompt speculators to test governments' resolve. Improvements in transaction technologies and the removal of capital controls will render this testing process virtually costless. Relative to the resources of the market, foreign support will necessarily remain limited. Hence radical increases in interest rates will be needed to prevent the exchange rate target from being violated. Even governments that would gladly maintain an exchange rate target

32. These pressures are clearly evident in the adaptations made recently by countries utilizing target zones. Chile, for example, has maintained an exchange rate band against the U.S. dollar since 1985, but with the progress of financial liberalization it has been forced to widen the band from 4 to 6, 10, and, in January 1992, 20 percent. Finland, Norway, and Sweden were forced to abandon their unilateral target zones in 1992. See Cukierman, Kiguel, and Leiderman (1993).

indefinitely in the absence of a speculative attack may feel compelled to abandon it by the costs of increased interest rates for debt service, the stability of the financial system, and the level of unemployment.

Countries will still be able to adjust their money supplies in response to exchange rate fluctuations. What they will not be able to guarantee is their ability to adjust monetary and other policies sufficiently to hit preannounced exchange rate targets. They will not be able to peg their exchange rates for significant periods of time. Regimes of pegged but adjustable rates like the Bretton Woods System and the EMS of the 1980s, in which governments attempted to hold their exchange rates within narrow bands except under exceptional circumstances, will no longer be viable. Crawling pegs, which differ only in that governments allow the prespecified band to shift each week or month, will be similarly problematic, as will exchange rate target zones.

Policymakers will therefore be forced to choose between floating exchange rates and monetary union. Floating rates can still be managed—governments will still be able to pursue policy rules in which exchange rate fluctuations trigger policy responses. What will not be feasible is a rule defined in terms of an exchange rate target that is to remain inviolable under all but exceptional circumstances.

The only options that remain, by this interpretation, are floating and monetary union. The next chapter considers the problem of choosing between them.

Chapter 6

The Optimum Currency Dilemma

C HANGES in technology, market structure, and politics, I have argued, will confront policymakers with an increasingly stark choice between floating exchange rates and monetary unification. The literature on optimum currency areas speaks to their dilemma.[1] It points to factors on which the choice between floating rates and monetary unification should turn, identifies countries for which that choice will be especially difficult, and suggests measures to temper their predicament.

The Economics of Optimum Currency Areas

Research on optimum currency areas has sought to identify characteristics of countries that shape the costs and benefits of a separate currency. The message of this literature is that a national currency whose supply can be independently controlled and whose rate of exchange against foreign currencies can therefore vary is most beneficial for countries experiencing different disturbances than their neighbors and consequently valuing monetary autonomy to facilitate adjustment. It is least beneficial for countries for which a separate currency implies the greatest increase in transaction costs.

1. Seminal contributions to the literature are Mundell (1961); McKinnon (1963); Kenen (1969). Early but still useful surveys are Ishiyama (1975); Tower and Willet (1976). A recent survey that touches on the political considerations I emphasize here is Goodhart (forthcoming).

Economic Size

Every individual, household, and city block faces idiosyncratic shocks. But no one would argue for a separate currency for every individual, household, or city block. A currency hardly functions as a useful unit of account if you are the only one who denominates prices in it. It hardly serves as a useful means of payment if you are the only one who accepts it in settlement.

For these reasons, monetary unification is attractive to smaller economies. The monetary unions currently in operation—the West African Monetary Union, the Central African Monetary Union, the East Caribbean Currency Area, Luxembourg-Belgium, and Liechtenstein-Switzerland—all involve relatively small economies.[2] The strongest result to emerge from empirical analyses of countries' choice of exchange rate regime is that small countries prefer to peg their exchange rates.[3]

Openness

Individuals, households, and city blocks are very open (they transact extensively with other individuals, households, and city blocks). If all exchange took place within city blocks (if the latter were closed to trade with one another), the transaction services of a separate currency for each block would not be inferior to those provided by a citywide money. The more transactions are conducted between blocks, however, the greater the resources that would have to be devoted to such operations as recalculating prices in local currency and exchanging currencies for one another. The more open is the economy, then, the less adequate are the means-of-payment and unit-of-account services provided by a separate currency. The more concentrated is a country's trade with a subset of partner countries, the more these means-of-payment and unit-of-account functions can be enhanced by the formation of a monetary union limited in geographical scope.

Working in the same direction, it is sometimes asserted, is the fact that more open economies possess smaller shares of nontraded goods in output, leaving them with less ability to use nominal exchange rate

2. A complete list would also include the use of the dollar by Liberia and Panama, and the Rand Monetary Area in southern Africa.
3. See Honkapohja and Pikkarainen (1992) for a survey of this literature and new results.

changes to alter the real exchange rate. A negative shock weakening a country's balance of payments may require shifting resources from nontraded to traded goods production, and a devaluation that raises import prices in domestic-currency units acts like a shift to daylight saving time to coordinate this adjustment; the smaller the nontraded goods sector, the weaker this mechanism, the argument runs.[4] Yet authors like Edwards and Corden find that even in very open economies changes in the nominal exchange rate affect the real exchange rate.[5] If openness is associated with a decision to forsake monetary autonomy for currency unification, this must reflect the savings in transaction costs rather than any irrelevance of exchange rate changes for adjustment.

Specialization

The larger are nation-specific shocks (the more asymmetric the distribution of macroeconomic disturbances across countries), the less adequate is a common monetary policy for adjustment, and the stronger is the case for a national currency to enhance monetary policy autonomy. Kenen took this insight, due to Mundell, and argued that countries in which output and employment are widely spread across sectors will have the least reason to float.[6] Insofar as industry-specific disturbances prevail, economies with broadly diversified production structures are least likely to experience disturbances requiring the kind of economy-wide adjustment that can be promoted by exchange rate changes. If one traded-goods sector booms when another slumps, a country possessing both can shift resources between them without any change in the exchange rate. An exchange rate change that alters the price of traded goods relative to domestic-currency-denominated labor costs is not helpful when some traded-goods prices have to rise and others have to fall.[7]

4. Thus the more consumer goods are imported, this argument goes, the more likely are workers to resist a devaluation-induced fall in the real consumption wage. The money illusion that the standard case for flexibility requires will not be available. Johnson (1970) calls this the "banana republic case."

5. See Edwards (1992); Corden (1993).

6. Kenen (1969); Mundell (1961).

7. The observation that diversified economies will find it least costly to peg must confront the fact that many highly specialized nations actually peg their exchange rates. The

Other Asymmetric Shocks

Sectoral specialization is not the only determinant of the incidence of asymmetric shocks.[8] Countries can experience nation-specific shocks to the velocity of circulation, to the stability of the banking system, to the level of wages, and to the productivity of labor. They can experience nationwide droughts, brutally cold winters, and (as in the case of Finland following the breakup of the Soviet Union) the collapse of their principal export markets. The question is whether possessing a national currency in fact eases adjustment to asymmetric shocks. Money, as a nominal variable, is most obviously useful as a response to nominal shocks. But if coordination failure is important, one can invoke the "daylight savings time" argument that monetary policy is also useful for adjusting to real disturbances. The observed behavior of governments is consistent with this view: the fact that Finland abandoned its policy of pegging to the ECU, devaluing in 1991 and floating its exchange rate in 1992, is hard to explain, for example, if one insists that monetary-cum-exchange-rate policy is useless for coping with real disturbances.

Insofar as domestic monetary policy is the source of shocks, a currency union may eliminate both the disturbance and the need for a response; conversely, if foreign monetary policy is the source, a floating exchange rate provides insulation. In a currency union, domestic velocity shocks are easily dispatched through the requisite inflow or outflow of the common currency, whereas foreign velocity shocks may subject a member of a currency union to a powerful monetary disturbance. Clearly the magnitude of asymmetric shocks is not a sufficient statistic for choosing between monetary unification and floating; it is necessary also to know the source of the disturbances.

---

petroleum-producing countries of the Middle East, which epitomize this category, peg to the dollar, as mentioned previously. This practice reflects the fact that such highly specialized economies are actually very open, and open economies have good reason to peg. Fixing the value of the national currency in terms of a single export commodity such as oil (that being the implication of adopting a floating rate) will subject households to severe fluctuations in their purchasing power *because* they depend on imports for consumption goods—that is, because the economy is so open. Clearly if the economy was both highly specialized and relatively closed, severe purchasing power fluctuations would not follow, and there would be little incentive for the government to stabilize the value of the currency in terms of some broader aggregate of goods (that is, to join a currency union).

8. Indeed Stockman (1987b) suggests that it is not one of the principal sources.

Factor Flexibility

Labor mobility was, along with the symmetry of shocks, the other consideration emphasized by Mundell. He argued that economies between which labor is mobile are good candidates for monetary union, since asymmetric shocks affecting one but not the others can be accommodated by labor flows between them. Blanchard and Katz confirm that labor flows between U.S. regions in fact play a major role in adjustment to disturbances within the U.S. economic and monetary union.[9]

In this context, *labor mobility* should be understood as shorthand for labor market flexibility generally. Incipient unemployment can be headed off by emigration or by currency depreciation, which reduces real wages, but it can can also be eliminated by a reduction in labor costs denominated in domestic currency (a fall in money wages). Thus an economy with relatively flexible labor markets (in the sense that wages vary absolutely and relative to those prevailing elsewhere) is the best candidate for monetary union.

This criterion is clearly related to the sectoral diversification of production. Only if labor is mobile internally can diversified economies accommodate sector- or region-specific shocks by shifting resources across sectors or regions.[10] Such economies can accommodate shocks by changing relative prices and costs only if wages and prices are flexible. Similarly a group of regions is most likely to constitute a smoothly adjusting currency union if their relative wages are flexible and workers display a propensity to move between them.

Labor market flexibility cannot be taken as exogenous with respect to international monetary arrangements any more than can monetary shocks. When the government is prepared to adjust the nominal exchange rate in response to shocks, workers and firms will have less reason to write contracts allowing for changes in money wages. If governments opt for monetary unification, workers and firms will realize that an inappropriate level of money wages can no longer be accommodated by nominal exchange rate adjustments and should be more likely to write contracts that deliver a greater degree of wage flexibility.[11]

9. See Blanchard and Katz (1992).

10. The obverse is also true: sectoral diversification may be needed to provide destinations to which labor has incentive to move; see Kenen (1969).

11. Italy's abolition of its *scala mobile* in advance of European monetary unification may be seen as an example of this tendency. Horn and Persson (1988) provide a model of this

Fiscal Flexibility

Labor mobility is an appropriate response to permanent disturbances. Relocation being costly, it may not make sense if disturbances
are short-lived. For such cases, theory points to external borrowing as
an efficient means of smoothing consumption and production. If
incomes fall temporarily, households, to sustain their consumption,
can borrow from other parts of the economic and monetary union.

Atkeson and Bayoumi show that households do in fact use capital
markets to insure against region-specific risks, but only to a limited
extent. Human capital is illiquid, contracting being discouraged by
private information and moral hazard. This creates a role for government to arrange the capital flows that private markets fail to mobilize.
Government can increase transfer payments to residents, running
budget deficits and financing them externally. Where governments are
best able to undertake this function, the costs of monetary unification
should be relatively low.[12]

The question is how much capacity governments possess to undertake this function. Sovereign borrowers retain the option of defaulting
and therefore cannot borrow without limit. In other words even if
governments are able to surmount private information problems,
moral hazard remains. The amount governments can borrow will
depend, moreover, on the conditions under which they operate.[13] The
more mobile are factors of production, the more footloose is a juris-
diction's tax base and the lower the level of debt at which it will find
itself rationed out of the capital market. Bayoumi, Goldstein, and
Woglom find that state governments in the United States are rationed
out of the market when their debt-to-state-product ratio exceeds
9 percent.[14]

---

idea. Bertola (1989) presents arguments suggesting that once exchange rates are immutably
fixed, workers will be more likely to respond to asymmetric shocks through interregional
migration. Alogoskoufis and Smith (1991) provide empirical evidence on the accommoda-
tion effects of different exchange rate regimes.

12. See Atkeson and Bayoumi (1991). This is a restatement of the well-known point in
international macroeconomics that the costs of forsaking a policy instrument (in the case of
monetary union, an independent monetary policy) will be low when another instrument is
available (in this case, fiscal policy).

13. Thus Bayoumi and Eichengreen (1994b) find that states with statutory or constitutional restrictions preventing them from running persistent deficits are able to borrow more
before being rationed out of the capital market.

14. See Bayoumi, Goldstein, and Woglom (1994).

Fears that this constraint may bind have led to suggestions of the need for systems of intergovernmental transfers in a monetary union. The argument is that long-term contracts between local jurisdictions to provide one another with regional coinsurance accomplish what decentralized markets cannot.[15] These long-term contracts take the form of systems of fiscal federalism, in which regions reduce their tax payments to the federal government and receive transfers from the federal authorities (and indirectly from other regional governments) when they suffer an asymmetric regional shock. Areas within which the institutions of fiscal federalism are well developed should therefore be inclined to opt for monetary unification.

Financial Development

Countries with underdeveloped financial markets will experience relatively high exchange rate volatility. A temporary disturbance that leads some investors to sell domestic-currency-denominated assets will cause the exchange rate to plummet if liquidity constraints or other market imperfections prevent other investors from purchasing those assets in anticipation of a subsequent recovery in their value. The absence of forward markets similarly renders it difficult for firms and households to hedge exchange risk. These are the circumstances under which exchange rate volatility will confer the greatest economic costs.

A common response to this problem is for the government to manage the exchange rate: to act as purchaser or seller of last resort of the relevant assets. The implication is that floating is most costly for countries with the least developed financial markets.[16]

Susceptibility to Inflation

Inflation weakens a currency's ability to provide store-of-value services and, when it reaches sufficient heights, eliminates it as a means of payment and unit of account. Hence one should expect countries most vulnerable to inflationary pressure to be most willing to sacrifice their monetary autonomy. This is the obvious explanation

15. This argument goes back to Ingram (1959).

16. It is noteworthy in this regard that one developing country that succeeded in floating independently for an extended period prior to its current troubles was Lebanon, a country with an unusually sophisticated financial system.

for why a country like Argentina established a rigid dollar link following its repeated failure to resist inflationary pressures, and one reason
why other European Community (EC) countries have linked their
currencies to the deutsche mark in the European Monetary System
(EMS).

The question, of course, is what prevents countries from abandoning their exchange rate peg when pressures to do so intensify, in the
manner of the United Kingdom and Italy in 1992? What lends credibility to the peg, in other words? As discussed in chapter 2, credibility
requires that the authorities incur a cost when failing to maintain the
exchange rate peg. They may offer themselves as hostages, promising
to resign if they renege on that pledge. But here too the question is
what lends credibility to that pledge—what prevents officials from
claiming that their failure to maintain the peg reflects a contingency
beyond their control?

Even when an exchange rate peg is credible, monetary unification
reopens the Pandora's box that pegging sought to close. A member of a
monetary union regains influence over the formulation of union-wide
monetary policy—the very thing it sought to renounce by delegating
control to the anchor country to which it pegged. One reason France
and other members of the EMS are proponents of European monetary
unification is that they seek to regain control of their monetary policies
from the German Bundesbank. What then prevents them from using
their influence, once reacquired, in the same inflationary manner as
before? By implication, the infeasibility of an exchange rate peg and the
unavoidable choice between floating and monetary unification introduce
difficult questions for countries whose choice is largely shaped by considerations of inflation vulnerability.

The Economics of Seigniorage

Seigniorage is a tax to which governments resort in their effort to
raise revenue. An efficiency-maximizing government will rely heavily
on this tax when other revenue sources are highly distortionary.
Hence countries with different economic structures will find it efficient to run different inflation-cum-monetary policies, a practice that
is not possible in a monetary union. In general, there will be a
trade-off between the discrepancy in national inflation rates consis-

tent with minimizing tax distortions and the minimization of trans-action costs due to the maintenance of separate currencies.[17]

Seigniorage accounts for a significant fraction of government re-ceipts in countries with underdeveloped financial markets, but for only a couple of points of gross national product (GNP) in the advanced industrial world. Such figures understate the economic benefits of domestic control of the inflation tax, however, insofar as the latter has insurance value. For example, highly indebted countries can issue debt at significantly reduced costs if investors know that there exists a purchaser of last resort, namely the central bank, to backstop the market in the event of a debt run.[18] A credible purchaser of last resort is sure to exist only when the central bank remains under domestic control. In contrast, if investors are unsure of the inclination of a common central bank in a monetary union to contain a debt run affecting one of its jurisdictions, they may demand a significant risk premium to hold its obligations.[19]

Recapitulation

The literature on optimum currency areas points to economic characteristics that should shape countries' choices between managed floating and monetary union. Small, open, specialized economies are most likely to opt for monetary union. The same will be true of countries with flexible labor markets and institutional means of relax-ing fiscal constraints. Countries immune to inflationary pressures but vulnerable to asymmetric macroeconomic disturbances, in contrast, may prefer to float.

The Politics of Optimum Currency Areas

This discussion of the literature on optimum currency areas paints the choice between floating and monetary union as one that is based on economic considerations. Political rather than eco-nomic factors in fact often seem to dictate the decision of which

17. See Canzoneri and Rogers (1990).
18. See McKinnon (forthcoming).
19. The insurance role of the inflation tax goes beyond containing runs on debt. More generally it gives governments a tax to use in bad states of the world. I take up this point in the next section on political factors.

tack to pursue.[20] Political objectives that can be attained through the maintenance of a separate currency or by the establishment of a monetary union may dominate any strictly economic calculus of costs and benefits. Moreover politics as much as markets shape the economic parameters emphasized in the literature on optimum currency area.

Money as a Symbol of Sovereignty

Sovereignty is one of those phenomena whose definition is more difficult to formulate than its importance is to deny. National currencies retain political value as a symbol of national sovereignty. In the former Soviet Union, for example, the Baltics and Ukraine, among other new countries, sought to replace the ruble with their own currencies to symbolize their national autonomy.[21] The German public hesitated to embrace European monetary unification when it realized that this entailed giving up the beloved deutsche mark.[22] Economists may despair that political symbolism can dominate economic calculus, but they must acknowledge that this is the case.

The Politics of Seigniorage

Even if seignorage revenues are usually small, monetary sovereignty may retain significant option value for a government. Sovereignty confers on a political entity the right to resist aggression from

20. Early recognition of this point can be found in Mintz (1970), upon which this section builds.

21. Similarly Russia desired to see them remain in the ruble zone to signal that its political influence still extended beyond the borders of the Russian Federation. It can be argued that with the rise of Russian inflation these other republics saw an economic logic to detaching themselves from a rapidly depreciating ruble. Even then, however, the symbols of nationalism continued to dominate discussion. Thus when an interstate bank for multilateral clearing between the successor states of the former Soviet Union was under negotiation in the first half of 1992, republics other than Russia resisted on grounds of symbolism the proposal that its accounts be denominated in rubles, even though as prospective debtors vis-à-vis the bank they stood to benefit from an arrangement under which debts would depreciate in nominal terms; see Eichengreen (1993b). Similarly, some regions *within* the Russian Federation striving for autonomy have periodically issued their own quasi-currency notes.

22. The tendency is not limited to Germany. Goodhart (forthcoming, p. 12) provides a telling quotation from Dr. George Cary, the Archbishop of Canterbury, speaking in February 1993: "I want the Queen's head on the banknotes. The point about national identity is a very important one. For me being British is deeply important. I don't want to become French or German." In the particular case of Germany, however, hesitancy to give up the deutsche mark may involve more than symbolism, as I discuss in chapter 7.

abroad. National defense in turn requires that the government be able to mobilize resources to resist attack. It follows that certain instruments of taxation, prominent among which is the inflation tax, are normally assigned to the national authorities to further their pursuit of this task. Seigniorage, obtained by issuing money, is the single most flexible instrument of taxation available to a government; in Goodhart's words, it is the revenue of last resort.[23] Money can be printed to pay soldiers, to purchase war matériel, and to underwrite the other costs of a war of national defense without having to wait for tax returns to be filed or for a foreign loan to be extended. Hence countries engaged in war commonly resort to the inflation tax, letting their currency depreciate and abandoning any commitment to an exchange rate peg.[24]

A flexible revenue source of last resort may also be of value when internal upheavals limit a government's ability to raise revenue from other sources. A natural disaster or insurrection must be dealt with expeditiously or it may threaten the stability of the government. Abandoning the option value entailed in the right to issue a national currency therefore presents significant risks for a sovereign nation.

For the same reasons monetary unification may be a credible way for governments to renounce extraterritorial ambitions. Abandoning national control over seigniorage by joining a monetary union diminishes the capacity to wage war.[25] This argument holds water, of course, only insofar as monetary unification is irreversible. If countries can reintroduce a national currency when tensions heighten, monetary unification does little to enhance their international political credibility. The question of whether monetary unification is irreversible was raised in chapter 3. The argument advanced there was that establishing a monetary union involves sunk costs that are lost in the event that the union is abandoned; these in turn serve as a barrier to exit that renders the union more credible than pegged exchange rates between distinct national currencies. But there may still be circumstances under which governments choose to write off sunk

23. See Goodhart (forthcoming).

24. De Kock and Grilli (1989) emphasize the connections among the outbreak of war, exceptional seigniorage needs, and shifts from pegged to floating exchange rates.

25. Readers inclined to dismiss this argument as farfetched would do well to reflect on twentieth-century European history. Memory of two devastating wars between Germany and France plays a nonnegligible role in the desire for economic and monetary unification between these two countries.

costs. Sunk costs that deter a government from depreciating its exchange rate in response to a recession may be inadequate to prevent it from withdrawing from the union in the event of a military conflict (witness the case of the former Yugoslavia). When the stakes are high, monetary unification may not credibly deter governments from initiating hostilities.

Money as a Political Bargaining Chip

The notion that a country may agree to monetary union not because the economic benefits outweigh the costs but rather because it is compensated for those costs by other, noneconomic benefits is a specific instance of the general argument that money can serve as a bargaining chip in international negotiations. This is one way of understanding German support for European monetary unification, for example. As the largest economy in Europe and the one least susceptible to inflationary pressures (not to mention the EC member state suffering the largest asymmetric economic shock, namely German unification), Germany of all EC member states had the least reason to be attracted to European monetary union on narrowly economic grounds. A popular explanation for its support for the Maastricht Treaty is that it offered to trade monetary union, for which it had little intrinsic desire, for an expanded foreign policy role within the context of an EC defense policy.[26] The implication is that cost-benefit calculations regarding monetary unification and floating rates only make sense when they are extended beyond narrowly defined economic factors.

Money and the Political Economy of Protection

In the same way that there can be cross-issue trades between countries over money and other issues, choices regarding international monetary policy can have significant spillovers into other domestic political arenas. Cooper, Williamson, and McKinnon argue that international monetary arrangements can have important implications for domestic trade politics, for example.[27] Exchange rate fluctuations, even when they benefit the nation as a whole, may so

26. See, for example, Eichengreen and Frieden (1993).
27. See Cooper (1984); Williamson (1985); McKinnon (1990).

injure particular sectors that the latter will seek to secure the imposition of protectionist measures to insulate them from further shifts.
The broadly based interests that reap diffuse benefits from free trade
may find it difficult to counter the highly concentrated interest groups
that suffer injury. Thus the U.S. decision to devalue the dollar in 1971
was influenced by mounting protectionist pressure in Congress (evidenced by the Burke-Hartke and Mills bills, for example) which in
turn reflected growing competitive difficulties. The U.S. decision to
abandon the freely floating dollar for the Plaza Accord in 1985 was
motivated by the fear that the currency's appreciation was generating
protectionist pressure from domestic producers undercut by import
competition. Wide exchange rate swings that lead to import surges
may similarly provoke a protectionist backlash, threatening the completion of Europe's internal market and the maintenance of historical
trade relations among the former Soviet republics.[28]

Countries and governments that value open markets may therefore
opt for monetary unification as a bulwark against protectionism. This
argument suggests that openness cannot be taken as a parameter
upon which to base optimum currency area calculations. Rather a
country's openness is endogenous with respect to the choice between
monetary union and floating, insofar as the latter shapes the political
economy of protection.

The Politics of Monetary Accountability

The legitimacy of political institutions in a democracy requires
accountability. To earn the respect and the cooperation of the citi-
zenry, political institutions must be seen as taking actions in the
long-term interest of the public. To ensure that they do so, decision
makers must be answerable to voters or their elected representatives.

28. On the former Soviet case see Eichengreen (1993b); Havrylyshyn and Williamson
(1991). On the European case the departure of sterling from the Exchange Rate Mechanism in September 1992 is instructive. The depreciation of the pound was not immediately
offset by changes in domestic-currency-denominated labor costs. This was one factor in the
Hoover Company's decision to terminate vacuum cleaner production in France in favor of
expanding its operations in Scotland. It encouraged Philips Electronics to cease producing
cathode ray tubes in its Dutch plant in favor of Britain. It helped to pursuade S. C. Johnson
& Son, a U.S. household products maker, to shift production from France to Britain. This
in turn led EC Commission President Delors to warn the British government that its
exchange rate policies were antagonizing other EC countries in a manner incompatible with
the privileges of the Single Market.

Thus as a provision of the Humphrey-Hawkins Act, which charges the U.S. government, including the Federal Reserve System, with pursuing congressionally mandated objectives such as the maintenance of full employment, the chairman of the Federal Reserve Board is required to testify before Congress on a regular basis. Other officials of the Federal Reserve System testify at Congress's request. If U.S. monetary officials fail to justify their actions their prerogatives may be threatened by bills modifying the statutory independence of the Federal Reserve System.

The situation in other countries is similar. In parliamentary systems, where changes in statute do not require the assent of both directly elected representatives and a separately elected chief executive, changes in statute may be even easier to engineer; the credibility of this threat may enhance the accountability of monetary policymakers.

Accountability is not the same thing as independence, of course: it is possible to make the monetary authority accountable for the pursuit of certain ultimate objectives (price stability and full employment, for instance) and at the same time free to choose its tactics for pursuing them. To return to the previous example, the Fed is both independent in the sense of enjoying statutory insulation from pressure to alter its tactics (its regulation of interest rates and monetary aggregates) and accountable in the sense that it will be called on the carpet if its tactics fail to deliver the desired results. This can be seen as an institutional solution to the time consistency problem that otherwise afflicts monetary policy, in which politicians with control of a discretionary monetary instrument cannot credibly commit to restraint. By appointing an agent (a conservative central banker) to act in the long-term interest of the principal (the polity), this time consistency problem can be ameliorated.[29] But this solution is politically acceptable and will deliver desirable results only if the agent, the central banker, is ultimately accountable in a political sense.

As soon as countries contemplate moving to monetary union, new questions of accountability arise. To which congress or parliament will the union-wide central bank be answerable? This has long been an issue in systems of pegged but adjustable exchange rates. Such systems are frequently based on the policy decisions of an anchor coun-

29. Seminal models of this time consistency problem are Kydland and Prescott (1977); Barro and Gordon (1983). The principal-agent solution to the problem was first analyzed by Rogoff (1985a).

try—the United States under the Bretton Woods system, Germany under the EMS. Those formulating policy in the anchor country are not directly accountable to the citizens of other countries; although the latter are free to voice their objections, the recipient of the message is under no obligation to listen. Of course countries participating in a pegged-rate system have an alternative to voice, namely exit. They can leave the system if they feel that the central bank setting the tone for monetary policy is not pursuing policies consistent with their objectives.

Assuming that monetary unification succeeds in attaining its objective of creating credible exit barriers, the scope for exit may be limited without enhancing the scope for voice. Monetary unification involves an international treaty; modifying that treaty to discipline renegade central bankers would therefore require the unanimous consent of the signatories, a formidable obstacle. Hence a country that feels that the common central bank is not pursuing objectives compatible with its national interest may have little opportunity to exercise either exit or voice.[30]

Politics and the Fiscal Concomitants of Monetary Union

The literature on optimum currency areas suggests that regions within which fiscal federalism is well developed are best positioned for monetary unification. Political rather than economic factors may pose the principal obstacle to the development of such arrangements. There is no mystery about the design of the institutions of federalism, in other words; the question is whether it is feasible to implement them prior to political unification.

The government's power to tax and spend is the essence of sovereignty. Whereas the power to issue a national money may have occasional value as a revenue source of last resort, the power to tax and spend is central to a government's pursuit of any objective. Governments therefore are understandably reluctant to compromise their fiscal prerogatives. Symptomatic of this fact is that in the EC, where the need for fiscal federalism as a concomitant of monetary union has long been acknowledged (for example in the MacDougall Report[31]) but political unification has not kept pace with economic integration,

30. I return to these points in the European context in chapter 7.
31. Commission of the European Communities (1977).

the European Union (EU) budget barely exceeds 1 percent of EU GNP. This limits the scope for fiscal federalism at the Union level. As long as separate sovereign jurisdictions remain, they will hesitate to cede their budgetary prerogatives, rendering difficult any attempt to develop the fiscal concomitants of monetary union.

Summary

The literature on optimum currency areas points to a small number of economic variables that should guide countries' choice between managed floating and monetary unification. It points to market imperfections and forms of market incompleteness to be corrected by governments seeking to establish a smoothly functioning monetary union. Ultimately, however, the binding constraints on solving those problems are more political than economic. The implication is that international monetary options in the twenty-first century will be shaped as much by political as by economic factors. The next two chapters apply these insights to Europe and other parts of the world in turn.

Chapter 7

European Prospects

O NE response to the argument of this book is that a choice between
monetary union and floating is no choice at all. Aside from small
countries lacking a history of monetary sovereignty, monetary unions
of separate nations have almost never been observed. From this
perspective, recent setbacks to efforts to establish a European monetary union should come as no surprise. If, for the reasons detailed in
chapter 5, compromise arrangements like the pegged but adjustable
exchange rates of the European Monetary System (EMS) will no
longer be feasible, and for the reasons discussed in the second half of
chapter 6 monetary unification without political unification is not in
the cards, the only viable option is some form of floating exchange
rates.

Recent events in Europe are at least superficially consistent with
this view. To determine whether this consistency is more than super-
ficial, this chapter analyzes the prospects for European monetary
unification in more detail. It finds more support for one of the two
propositions in the preceding paragraph than for the other. Although
recent European experience unambiguously confirms the lack of
viability of policy rules framed in terms of contingent exchange rate
targets, it does not establish the infeasibility of monetary unification.

A Case Study of the Infeasibility of Exchange Rate Targets

By the beginning of the 1990s European policymakers had grown
convinced that there existed a compromise between floating exchange

rates and monetary unification—a compromise of sufficient durability to bridge the transition to European monetary union. This was the European Monetary System of pegged but adjustable exchange rates. From early 1987 it became the European Monetary System of pegged exchange rates, as no further realignments took place from January of that year until the crises starting in the summer of 1992 that affirmed the fragility of the EMS.

A Précis of the Crisis

The currency crises of 1992–93 are sufficiently familiar to require only the briefest of summaries here. Denmark's June 2, 1992, referendum on the Maastricht Treaty, in which the treaty suffered a narrow defeat, opened the first episode of instability.[1] The Italian lira, which had joined the narrow band on January 8, 1990, quickly fell toward its lower limit despite intramarginal intervention, reflecting Italy's large budget deficit and political disarray. The three currencies of the wide band (the British pound, the Spanish peseta, and the Portuguese escudo) then weakened.[2] These events occurred against the backdrop of mounting exchange rate tensions in the Nordic countries, depreciation of the U.S. dollar (which fell by 17 percent against the deutsche mark between mid-March and early September), and weakness of the yen against the EMS currencies.

Pressure mounted in August and September with the approach of France's September 20 referendum on the Maastricht Treaty. On August 26 the pound fell to its Exchange Rate Mechanism (ERM) floor. Other ERM members intervened in support of their currencies. On September 8, the Finnish markka's ECU link was severed, heightening investors' doubts about the sustainability of other exchange rate

1. A longer account would explain how the EMS crisis was preceded by exchange rate turmoil at the fringes of the European Community (EC). In the second half of 1991, Finland had experienced capital outflows caused by the collapse of its Soviet trade and a domestic banking crisis. The Bank of Finland, which had maintained an ECU peg, was forced on November 14, 1991, to devalue the markka by 12 percent. Pressure spilled over to Sweden, which exported many of the same products and maintained a similar ECU peg, forcing the Riksbank to raise its marginal lending rate by six points, to 17.5 percent. But notwithstanding these events, there was a striking absence of difficulties in the EC itself toward the beginning of 1992. For details, see Eichengreen (1993d).

2. The narrow band allowed fluctuations of plus or minus 2.25 percent in participating currencies. Certain junior members were permitted wider bands of plus or minus 6 percent, although the Maastricht Treaty required candidates for monetary union to bring their currencies into the narrow band.

pegs. Currency traders turned to the Swedish krona; the Riksbank, to defend its ECU peg, was forced to raise its marginal lending rate to triple-digit levels.

The lira was the leading target within the ERM. Despite the Bank of Italy's decision to permit a rise in short-term rates to more than 30 percent and heavy intervention by Germany, Holland, and Belgium, whose currencies reached their maximum permissible divergence against Italy, the lira was devalued by 7 percent against other ERM currencies on September 13.[3] The first discontinuous realignment in five years removed any doubt that changes in ERM exchange rates were still possible, and the small size of the German interest rate cut that followed the Italian action placed the burden of adjustment squarely on the weak-currency countries. Pressure mounted on Britain, Spain, Portugal, and Italy. Despite further interest rate increases and intervention, British ERM membership was suspended on September 16. Italy announced to the EC Monetary Committee that the inadequacy of its reserves in the face of speculative pressure forced it to suspend foreign exchange market intervention and to allow the lira to float; the Committee authorized a 5 percent devaluation of the peseta.

In the subsequent period speculative pressure was felt by the French franc, the Danish krone, and the Irish punt. The Bank of France raised interest rates, and fears for the stability of the franc spilled over to Belgian currency markets. Though the French franc remained above the bottom of its band, the Bank of France and the Bundesbank were compelled to intervene.[4] The Spanish authorities reimposed deposit requirements on banks lending for the purpose of financing certain currency swaps, while threats to the escudo and the punt induced Portugal and Ireland to tighten the capital controls that they had been permitted to retain under derogations granted them by the provisions of the Single European Act.

The crisis deepened following Sweden's decision to abandon its ECU peg on November 19 because of the government's failure to obtain all-party support for fiscal austerity measures.[5] Pressure spread

3. This was actually accomplished through a 3.5 percent devaluation of the lira and a 3.5 percent revaluation of other ERM currencies.

4. A total of 160 billion francs (about $32 billion) was spent in the currency's defense in the week ending on September 23; see Bank for International Settlements (1993, p. 188).

5. Massive reserve losses were incurred in the six days preceding the devaluation, reportedly amounting to $26 billion, or more 10 ten percent of Sweden's gross national product (GNP); see Bank for International Settlements (1993, p. 188).

to Denmark, forcing its central bank to raise interest rates, and to Iberia. Although the krone was successfully defended, it proved necessary to devalue the peseta and the Portuguese escudo by 6 percent. Norway was forced to abandon its unilateral ECU peg on December 10, and pressure spread to Ireland and France. Though the franc was successfully defended, the punt was not. In the face of Ireland's removal of capital controls on January 1, 1993 (as mandated by its derogation to the Single European Act) and the continued descent of the pound sterling (fueled by a series of British interest rate cuts), increases in Irish market rates to triple-digit levels did not suffice. (Between September 16 and the end of the year, sterling declined by 13 percent against the deutsche mark.) The punt was devalued by 10 percent within the ERM on January 30. The Danish krone and then the Belgian franc came under renewed attack, but this was successfully rebuffed.

The third crisis afflicted Spain and Portugal in May 1993. The approach of elections heightened uncertainty about the identity and orientation of the prospective Spanish government. Weakness of the peseta and extensive reserve losses prompted a further 8 percent devaluation. Although Portugal was subject to no such electoral uncertainty, it felt it necessary (and the Monetary Committee agreed) to devalue the escudo by 6.5 percent to prevent the country's competitive position from being eroded by the actions of its Spanish neighbor.

The last crisis, in July 1993, put an end to Europe's policy of pegging exchange rates within narrow bands. France's inflation rate remained several percentage points lower than Germany's, and the competitiveness of its exports was not in doubt. Nonetheless, massive franc sales led to unprecedented volumes of intervention. Smaller European countries also suffering from the recession, whose export competitiveness would have been significantly undercut by a French devaluation (Belgium, Denmark, Spain, and Portugal), saw their currencies fall to their ERM floors.

Following intensive negotiations over the last weekend of July, during which suspension of the ERM, temporary withdrawal of Germany from the EMS, and a variety of other options were mooted, European governments opted for widening the narrow band from 2.25 to 15 percent. This face-saving step retained the facade of the ERM while acknowledging the infeasibility of the narrow band.

Explaining the Crisis

Some have argued that the collapse of narrow bands reflected inadequate dedication to the harmonization of national economic policies, not the intrinsic fragility of pegged rates.[6] In this view, certain countries—most prominently Italy but also Spain and the United Kingdom—failed to restrain inflation and maintain the competitiveness required for external balance.

Although competitiveness problems are undoubtedly part of the story, it is far from clear that the 1992 crisis could have been averted had such countries more faithfully restrained aggregate demand. More restraint would have meant more unemployment; this would have intensified the pressure for governments to relax the stance of policy, even if doing so created exchange rate instability. Anticipations of this inevitability might have only increased the probability of a crisis.[7]

In addition the competitiveness explanation sits uneasily with the observed behavior of forward exchange rates. If observers attached a high probability to policy shifting in a more expansionary direction, why then did the one-year-ahead forward rates of most of the ERM currencies that were attacked starting in September 1992 not move outside their ERM bands in July or August? Of the major ERM currencies only the Italian lira and the Danish krone (not surprisingly, given that Danish voters had already demonstrated their reservations about the monetary provisions of the Maastricht Treaty) saw their forward rates move significantly outside their fluctuation bands prior to September.

Charles Wyplosz and I have suggested that this crisis may have reflected precisely the kind of self-fulfilling speculative attack discussed in chapter 3. Absent the attack, ERM countries—for example

6. This was the reaction of official bodies, echoed in academic commentary by, among others, Branson (1993); Dornbusch (1993).

7. Ozkan and Sutherland (1994), as already mentioned, provide a theoretical analysis of this mechanism. The association of exchange rate tensions with the shifting prospects for ratification of the Maastricht Treaty lends support to this view. If the treaty was not going to be ratified it no longer paid for countries to bear the burden of unemployment now as a way of demonstrating their commitment to participate in the monetary union later. From this perspective it is no coincidence that exchange market tensions first surfaced when the Danes rejected the treaty in their June referendum, that they intensified each time an opinion poll was released documenting the extent of opposition to ratification in France, or that they peaked preceding France's September 20 referendum.

Britain—would have been willing to maintain the policies of austerity required to defend their ERM pegs indefinitely, enduring the costs of unemployment in return for the benefits of exchange rate stability. Once attacked, however, they were forced to increase interest rates yet further to defend the currency, and this raised the cost-benefit ratio of the policy. The attack therefore induced them to abandon policies of supporting an exchange rate peg that they would have been able and willing to maintain indefinitely in the absence of speculative pressure. Aware of these incentives, speculators had a good reason to undertake a self-fulfilling attack. Countries where sensitivity to unemployment was greatest, where banking systems were weakest (implying the greatest risk of bank failures due to increased interest rates), and where debt-to-income ratios were highest (implying the greatest increase in fiscal burdens) were most vulnerable to such self-fulfilling attacks.[8]

The July 1993 attack on the French franc is consistent with this view. France had low inflation and no problem of export competitiveness. The government went to great lengths to signal its commitment to the policies needed to defend the *franc fort*. Absent a speculative attack, there is reason to think that the prevailing exchange rate could have been maintained indefinitely. However, when an attack came, requiring further interest rate increases and additional unemployment to defend the franc, the government was unable to comply. The Bank of France, having raised domestic rates only modestly, exhausted its reserves on the final Friday of July.[9] The abandonment of the narrow band followed.

By this interpretation, recent European experience illustrates the vulnerability of pegged but adjustable exchange rates to speculative attacks even when governments are committed to policies consistent

8. See Eichengreen and Wyplosz (1993). In addition, Wyplosz and I suggest that the provisions of the Maastricht Treaty increased the scope for self-fulfilling attacks. The convergence criteria that must be met by countries qualifying for monetary union include one requiring them to keep their exchange rate within the normal, narrow EMS fluctuation band without "severe tensions" for the two years preceding entry. Hence an attack forcing a devaluation might disqualify a country from participating in Europe's monetary union. This in turn would remove the government's incentive to persist with policies whose benefits resided in qualifying the country for monetary union. A rational government might shift toward more accommodating policies only if attacked, and knowledge of this fact could give traders the incentive to undertake such an attack.

9. In fact, intervention *more than* exhausted its reserves, as the Bank engaged in extensive foreign borrowing.

with the prevailing level of the exchange rate. It underscores the problems of attempting to maintain pegged but adjustable rates and narrow target zones in an environment of political uncertainty and high international capital mobility.

Prospects for European Monetary Unification

The episodes just described reveal flaws in the Maastricht blueprint for the transition to monetary union. Can this transition strategy simply be revised, for example at the Intergovernmental Conference already scheduled for 1996? Or is the goal no longer viable?

The Goal

The European Union (EU) more closely approximates than most other regional groupings the criteria for an optimum currency area. Although most EU member states are not the kind of small countries for which the costs of floating are prohibitive, neither are they the kind of continental economies, like that of the United States, for which floating does little to erode the value of money services.[10] EU members are open and trade heavily with one another. More than 20 percent of EU GNP is exported; the comparable figure for the United States, Canada, and Mexico is less than 10 percent. Of the trade of EU countries 60 percent is with other member states; the comparable figure for the United States, Canada, and Mexico is only about one-third. More than half of all foreign investment received by EU members comes from other member states; the analogous figure for the United States, Canada, and Mexico is about 25 percent.[11] For all these reasons arguments for a regional monetary grouping based on savings in transaction costs have particular salience in Europe.[12]

10. The European Commission shows that currency conversion costs amount to several percentage points of the transaction for individuals and small firms and estimates that these average about 0.5 percent of gross domestic product for the Community as a whole; see Emerson and others (1992, p. 21).

11. See Bayoumi and Eichengreen (1994a, table 4).

12. An exception to this generalization is inflation vulnerability. West European nations are plausibly less susceptible to inflationary pressures than many countries of Latin America, Eastern Europe, and the former Soviet Union, notwithstanding the impetus that the desire to resist inflation lent to policies of pegging to the deutsche mark in the early 1980s. Collins and Giavazzi (1993) document the shift in public attitudes toward inflation that subsequently occurred.

European experience provides a reminder that many of these variables are endogenous to the choice of international monetary regime. As recently as thirty years ago, trade among the twelve members of today's EU accounted for only 40 percent of their total trade. Such variables should not therefore be taken as unalterable constraints on the choice of international monetary arrangement. But European experience also indicates that significant changes in these magnitudes can only be effected over a period of decades. They remain significant considerations in the short run.

Recall that the greater the prevalence of asymmetric shocks, the higher the option value of monetary policy autonomy. The appropriate characterization of such shocks in Europe is not clear. Both France and Germany possess automotive industries, steel industries, and electronics industries. Since the same industries operate in many European countries, sector-specific shocks will affect these countries in similar ways. Moreover since the degree of sectoral specialization in EU countries is no higher than that characterizing different U.S. regions,[13] insofar as regional specialization connotes region-specific shocks it does not obviously represent a prohibitive barrier to European monetary integration.[14]

Sectoral specialization is not a sufficient statistic for the incidence of disturbances, of course, since it is possible for shocks to be country- rather than sector-specific. Bayoumi and Eichengreen compare (1) the correlation of the GDP growth rates of other EU members with Germany's growth rate over the last thirty years with (2) the correlation of the growth rates of other U.S. regions with that for the U.S. Mid-East. The latter correlation averages 0.68, the former correlation a somewhat smaller 0.58. Although the U.S. figure is higher, the differential is not large; it does not suggest that asymmetric shocks will be an insurmountable problem for Europe.[15]

But output movements are not the same as disturbances: the former conflate information on shocks and responses to them. Bayo-

13. In fact it is lower; see Krugman (1993); Bini Smaghi and Vori (1992).

14. Here I follow the practice of the literature, which takes as a metric the United States, where the incidence of shocks and the extent of labor flexibility and fiscal integration are consistent with the operation of a viable monetary union.

15. See Bayoumi and Eichengreen (1993). Similarly Cohen and Wyplosz (1989) transform real GDP data for France and Germany into sums and differences, interpreting movements in the sums as symmetric disturbances and movements in the differences as asymmetric disturbances. They find that symmetric shocks are much larger than asymmetric shocks. Weber (1990) applies their approach to other EC countries, reaching similar conclusions.

umi and Eichengreen use a technique of Blanchard and Quah to recover disturbances and responses from time series of output and prices.[16] The correlation of other EU countries' permanent disturbances with Germany's averages only 0.33, compared to 0.46 in the United States, whereas the correlation of the other EC countries' temporary disturbances with Germany's averages only 0.18, compared to 0.37 in the United States. In contrast to analyses of the raw data these findings suggest that asymmetric disturbances are more pervasive in Europe than within the United States.[17]

The emphasis in the optimum currency area literature on labor market flexibility provides additional grounds for caution. Wages are less flexible in Europe than in North America: a study by the Organization for Economic Cooperation and Development concludes that the elasticity of wages with respect to unemployment was lower in every one of eight EU countries than in the United States.[18] Observed rates of migration both between European countries and within them are lower than migration rates between regions of the United States, and econometric studies confirm that European migration is less responsive to wage and unemployment differentials.[19]

A final cause for caution is the absence in Europe of institutional mechanisms for fiscal coinsurance. Monetary union in the United States and Canada is supported by systems of fiscal federalism that offset about 20 percent of a cyclical shortfall in regional income (relative to income in the rest of the federation). Most of this transfer takes place through a decline in regional tax payments to the federal center when local incomes fall, a smaller portion through a rise in federal spending locally.[20] The absence of comparable arrangements

16. See Bayoumi and Eichengreen (1992, 1993); Blanchard and Quah (1989). This involves transforming the residuals from regressions of growth and inflation rates on lagged values of themselves, subject to the assumption that permanent disturbances affect both output and price levels in the long run but that temporary disturbances have no long-term output effect.

17. Chamie, DeSerres, and Lalonde (1994) extend this methodology in various directions but reach the same conclusion.

18. See Organization for Economic Cooperation and Development (1989).

19. I report such evidence for the United Kingdom and Italy in Eichengreen (1992b). A study by Antolin and Bover (1993) provides evidence for Spain, again consistent with the hypothesis of low interregional labor mobility in Europe.

20. The first empirical analysis, that of Sala-i-Martin and Sachs (1992), used data for U.S. census regions to relate tax and transfer payments to movements in pretax personal income, both measured relative to the national average. They found that federal

in Europe suggests that monetary union there may be characterized by more pervasive regional problems.

To what extent will these obstacles to monetary unification change over time? Econometric analysis of the incidence of shocks is necessarily based on historical correlations. Yet the structure generating those correlations is likely to change with the completion of the Single Market and monetary union. Temporary disturbances attributable to demand management policy should become more symmetric following European monetary union, since monetary policies will converge across participating countries, whereas permanent or supply disturbances will have less tendency to change; if anything they will grow less symmetric as sectoral specialization is reinforced. The government subsidies and import barriers that have supported the existence of an automobile industry in every large European country, for example, will be eroded by integration. Sectors characterized by strong agglomeration economies will have an incentive to consolidate production. These responses may magnify country-specific shocks, but completion of the internal market will also encourage intraindustry trade. In sectors characterized by scale economies and product differentiation different varieties of the same product may be produced in a growing number of European countries. Thus intraindustry trade may lead to an even greater duplication of industries across EU countries, damping region-specific shocks.[21]

Real wages in Europe may become more flexible with monetary union[22]; Italy's abolition of the *scala mobile*, as mentioned in chap-

---

tax liabilities decline by roughly 25 cents for every dollar by which regional income falls short of national income and that inward transfers rise by roughly 10 cents. Bayoumi and Masson (1991) consider both the United States and Canadian fiscal systems. They first regress each region's per capita income net of taxes and transfers on its per capita personal income inclusive of taxes and transfers. This equation measures the relationship between personal income before and after federal fiscal flows, with the slope coefficient capturing the size of the offset. For the United States, their coefficient of 0.78 indicates that, on average, federal fiscal flows reduce regional income inequalities by 22 cents on the dollar. They then estimate the same regression after differencing the variables to remove the equalization effect. Regressions on the differenced data produce a coefficient of 0.69, suggesting that the stabilization of short-term fluctuations (31 cents on the dollar) is even stronger than the overall effect. For Canada, Bayoumi and Masson find evidence of a substantial equalization effect: nearly 40 cents on each dollar. Their estimate of the insurance effect, although slightly smaller than that for the United States, is nonetheless substantial.

21. Emerson and others (1990); Gros and Thygesen (1992); Bini Smaghi and Vori (1992).

22. See, for example, Horn and Persson (1988).

ter 6, is indicative of this tendency, although few observers would predict that real wages will quickly acquire the flexibility characteristic of American labor markets.[23] Although European integration will enhance both the incentive and the capacity for labor to migrate, the question is to what extent such immigration will actually take place. Linguistic and cultural differences will remain. It seems farfetched to assume that European labor mobility will rise to American levels.

What of the scope for fiscal coinsurance? The European Union's budget is little more than 1 percent of EU GNP, as noted previously, and the largest share is devoted to the Common Agricultural Policy, leaving it unavailable for other uses. Much of the remainder is allocated to the Structural Funds, which are targeted at low-income regions within the Union and hence provide equalization rather than insurance.[24]

Italianer and Pisani-Ferry (1992) propose a program tailored to replicate the coinsurance effects of fiscal federalism without requiring a radical increase in the size of the EU budget. Under their scheme, when a member's unemployment rose relative to the EU average, so would its transfer receipts. Assuming that transfers are capped once the change in unemployment differentials reaches two percentage points, this proposal would require adding to the EU budget no more than 0.25 percent of EU GDP (assuming that the historical relationship between national unemployment rates continues to prevail). The program would offset about 20 percent of a temporary decline in a region's relative income. This offset is less than that seen in the United States, where interstate fiscal transfers depend not on relative unemployment rates but on fluctuations in both absolute and relative incomes. Nevertheless a reasonable degree of regional coinsurance could be provided without a revolu-

23. Blanchard and Muet (1993), for example, find that the growing credibility of France's commitment to pegging the franc to the deutsche mark was accompanied by little increase in real wage flexibility.

24. Gordon (1991) estimates that a $1 fall in a member state's per capita income increases its Structural Fund receipts by at most 1 U.S. cent. At Maastricht a coalition of four low-income countries led by Spain received assurances that these funds would be increased. But proposals to increase significantly the size of the Community budget, a prerequisite for such a step, subsequently ran into resistance. The Structural Funds would have to be increased by an order of magnitude to provide regional coinsurance on the U.S. or Canadian scale.

tion in European fiscal relations as long as a specific program is dedicated to the task.[25]

The real obstacles to such a program are political, not economic. Large-scale fiscal federalism (the transfer of significant revenue-raising capacity to the central authority) requires political integration. Residents of member countries lack a European Parliament with meaningful powers to hold accountable the technocrats who oversee the EU's budget. It is true that some budgetary decisions are made by a committee composed of national finance ministers who are accountable to their constituents, but residents of any one EU country may find their elected representative, if he is isolated, unable to influence decisionmaking. The same is true of some dissenting regions within existing federations, of course, but such regions can be compensated by concessions in other issue areas. The Union's limited hegemony in Europe's legal, cultural, and foreign policies, however, limits the scope for offering such matching concessions. All this renders unlikely the large-scale transfer of national fiscal functions to Brussels prior to the establishment of significant direct democracy.

A modest program targeted directly at the coinsurance problem, à la Italianer and Pisani-Ferry, is more realistic politically. The EU has, after all, agreed to the creation of a Common Agricultural Policy, in which some 0.75 percent of the Union's GDP is spent on a system of agricultural transfers that redistribute income across sectors and countries. The Structural Funds are a similar kind of transfer program. Spending 0.25 percent of EU GDP on a program of fiscal coinsurance does not seem unrealistic in this light. But there exist well-defined constituencies for the Common Agricultural Policy (Europe's farmers) and for the Structural Funds (low-income countries as well as regions sensitive to immigration). The potential beneficiaries of regional coinsurance are more difficult to characterize. Countries with extensive systems of fiscal federalism did not establish these with regional coinsurance in mind; rather their fiscal structures evolved in that direction with the growth of the federal government, a

25. See Italianer and Pisani-Ferry (1992). Obviously it would be necessary to design such a program to minimize moral hazard (for example to discourage countries from taking actions like raising the minimum wage and thus possibly increasing unemployment, which they would be more inclined to do if higher unemployment brought in transfers from the rest of the European Union). This problem might be addressed by strengthening coordination of social policies. For a more detailed discussion of the Italianer–Pisani-Ferry proposal see Reichenbach and others (1993).

concomitant of political unification and centralization. For Europe to create a system that provided the insurance effects of fiscal federalism prior to forming a monetary union would be unprecedented.

The political constraints on European monetary union are also evident when one considers the governance of the European Central Bank (ECB). In the ECB as constituted under the Maastricht Treaty "the Europeans have created an instrument that would greatly widen the already large democratic gap. The Maastricht agreement would create a powerful body of Platonic guardians to look after monetary affairs, effectively accountable to no one, yet with strong influence on the course of economic affairs."[26] Although ECB officials may be required to testify before the European Parliament, that institution has little power to hold them accountable. The ECB's independence could only be modified by amending an international treaty, subject to veto by any of the signatories, and not by the European Parliament.[27]

These problems are one source of skepticism in Germany about the desirability of a European Central Bank. History renders Germans hypersensitive to inflation. Although the central bank statute embedded in the Maastricht Treaty should insulate the ECB from political pressure every bit as effectively as the Bundesbank Law insulates the German central bank, and although the treaty singles out price stability as a paramount goal of policy, lack of accountability provides little recourse in the event that the ECB fails to pursue that goal with adequate dedication. Here again it is the political constraints that bind: monetary union without political union to provide accountability and safeguards leaves Germans in the street hesitant to give up their deutsche marks for ECUs.

That political constraints are the binding ones does not mean that they are insurmountable. Indeed some political pressures cut in the other direction. Money as a symbol of sovereignty and a source of seigniorage, although not irrelevant, figures less prominently in West-

26. Cooper (1992, p. 15). Similar points are made by Kenen (1992).

27. A decision in 1993 by the German Constitutional Court on the validity of Germany's ratification of the Maastricht Treaty seemed to hold out the possibility that Germany, having joined the European monetary union, would be entitled unilaterally to withdraw at a later date. Even if this interpretation is correct, the fact that withdrawal might require withdrawing from the EU itself (since the Maastricht Treaty is a series of amendments to the Treaty of Rome, the document establishing the European Community), renders this option less practicable.

ern Europe than in other parts of the world. For both negative and positive reasons (memories of two twentieth-century wars and the rapid progress of the EC, respectively), war between EU countries borders on the inconceivable. Insofar as the capacity to raise seigniorage retains option value, that value resides in Europe's relations with the rest of the world; hence vesting responsibility for controlling it in a European Central Bank does not pose a problem. In summary peaceful relations among EU member states make monetary union a more realistic short-term possibility in Europe than in other parts of the world.

The existence of the EU also expands the scope for monetary union by creating possibilities for trade-offs across issue areas. A legacy of World War II is that Germany is constrained in playing a significant foreign policy role unilaterally; the growth of the EU, including limited steps in the direction of political integration, makes it possible to contemplate an EU foreign policy within whose context Germany could acquire a foreign policy role. Other countries more interested in monetary union could offer to grant this to Germany in return for concessions on monetary union.[28]

The scope for trade-offs across issue areas is also evident in the economic sphere, where EU member states are pursuing initiatives on everything from barriers to commodity and factor flows to technical standards, deposit insurance, and immigration control. The issue boils down to whether monetary union is a political prerequisite for economic union. Completing the Single Market in commodities and factors of production, economists agree, will deliver significant efficiency gains. Even if the majority of those gains are technically obtainable despite the maintenance of separate national currencies, a single currency may be required to suppress the political resistance that economic integration would otherwise provoke. The argument runs as follows. The more integrated are national markets, the larger are the import surges that accompany exchange-rate-induced shifts in relative prices, and the greater is the pain experienced by affected firms and workers. The complaints over competitive depreciation and exchange dumping that followed the departure of sterling and the lira

28. This point is illustrated by the crisis in the former Yugoslavia. The Community's failure to develop a coherent response to the crisis undoubtedly cooled German leaders' enthusiasm for an EU foreign policy, a reaction that in turn strengthened their resistance to monetary union.

from the EMS in 1992 illustrate the point. Monetary union that prevents "capricious" exchange rate swings, thereby ruling out the associated costs, may be necessary to prevent affected sectors from lobbying against economic integration and to ensure the political viability of the Single Market process.[29] In addition, the intricate set of transfers and side payments that makes the Single Market acceptable to all the countries concerned is more difficult to administer when exchange rates vary.[30]

Thus the fact that the EU has made considerable progress and has future ambitions on the economic integration front provides a political logic for its continued pursuit of monetary union.

The Transition

The Maastricht Treaty specified a transition to occur in stages. Stage I was to be marked by the removal of capital controls, the reduction of international inflation and interest rate differentials, and the increasing stability of intra-European exchange rates. Stage II, which commenced at the beginning of 1994, is to be characterized by the further convergence of national economic policies and the creation of a temporary entity, the European Monetary Institute, to coordinate member country monetary policies and study the logistics of moving to monetary union. If during Stage II the Council of Ministers, made up of ministers of economics or finance from each national government, decides that the relevant number of member countries meet the preconditions for monetary union, it may recommend that the Council of Heads of State vote on whether to inaugurate Stage III—monetary union—establishing an independent European central bank and transferring to it responsibility for the conduct of monetary policy.

29. This is not to deny that shifts in relative prices can also adversely affect sector- and region-specific factors of production in a monetary union. But figures 2-1 and 2-2 highlight the additional dislocations that can occur between different monetary areas. With the passage of time, economic and monetary integration can lead to the growth of portfolio diversification across regions, which diminishes the welfare effects.

30. The Common Agricultural Policy—whose administration required the creation of synthetic "green exchange rates" to prevent the attempt to establish domestic-currency-denominated floors on agricultural prices in all member states from being disrupted by swings in market rates—is a particularly clear illustration of the general point. The argument is developed in more depth by Giavazzi and Giovannini (1989).

The treaty requires EU heads of state or government to meet no later than December 31, 1996, to assess whether a majority of EU member countries satisfy the conditions for monetary union; if they determine that a majority do they may set a date for the beginning of Stage III. If no date has been set by the end of 1997 Stage III will begin on January 1, 1999, as long as at least two countries qualify.[31] The conditions that participating countries must meet include interest rate stability, price stability, budget balance, and—critically for present purposes—exchange rate stability. Countries must hold their exchange rates within the normal EMS fluctuation bands without "severe tensions" for two years prior to the decision of the Council of Ministers. Thus the Maastricht Treaty envisaged a period of at least two years but probably longer over which exchange rates were pegged, capital controls were absent, and the potential for independent national monetary policies remained. This is precisely what the central argument of this book suggests is infeasible. That the EMS was shattered by a foreign exchange crisis in 1992, barely two years after the final removal of capital controls, and that a second such crisis less than a year later forced the abandonment of the narrow-band EMS is no coincidence from this point of view.

Must the Maastricht strategy therefore be altered? One response is to say that the problem was solved in July 1993 when the narrow ERM band (2.25 percent on either side of the central parity) was widened to 15 percent on either side of the central rate. Since this zone is so wide and governments' commitment to its defense is unlikely to be tested, it creates no problems of sustainability. Countries can claim to satisfy the Maastricht preconditions for monetary union insofar as 30 percent is now the width of the normal ERM band. Nothing prevents them from leaping from a system of exchange rates free to fluctuate within broad bands directly to monetary union.

In fact most European leaders and German leaders in particular continue to see an extended period during which exchange rates are pegged within the "normal" EMS bands—by which they mean 2.25 percent—as an essential prelude to monetary union. They see it as an indispensable opportunity for potential participants to demonstrate their willingness and ability to live with the consequences for policy of a single currency. They reject calls for leaping directly from wide

31. In the event that fewer than two countries qualify Stage II presumably will continue.

bands to monetary union. If the EU sticks with wide bands and significant exchange rate swings result, moreover, the latter may be corrosive of the Single Market project. With countries complaining of competitive depreciation and exchange dumping, the progress of European integration will slow. Insofar as EU countries prefer monetary union over floating mainly because the former is necessary politically to sustain the creation of a single market, were the integration process to be halted or reversed the main motivation to shift from floating to monetary union would be removed.

If to avoid derailing the Single Market project the Community therefore attempts to restore the narrow bands of the pre-1993 EMS, it is likely to confront the same problem of instability as before. For all the reasons outlined in chapter 5 there is no reason to think that, in an environment of political uncertainty and free capital mobility, pegged but adjustable exchange rates will be more viable in the future than in the recent past. This belief has led to proposals for buttressing the stability of pegged but adjustable rates over the transition by placing a transaction tax on purchases and sales of foreign currency or requiring non-interest-bearing deposits of all financial institutions lending domestic currency to nonresidents.[32]

As explained in chapter 5 opportunities to evade such measures increase with economic integration. In the prevailing European view, moreover, a foreign exchange transaction tax or deposit requirements would be inconsistent with the desire for financial liberalization and integration. Whatever the validity of these reservations, the problem of viable alternatives remains. If the premise of this book is correct, the EU possesses only two options for completing the transition to monetary union: leaping there directly from floating (presumably within wide bands), or undertaking a more gradual transition under cover of a foreign exchange transactions tax or deposit requirements on bank lending to nonresidents. A rational choice between these alternatives should hinge on which option is viewed as less corrosive to completing Europe's internal market.

---

32. A tax or deposit requirement on bank lending to nonresidents would make it more costly for speculators to borrow the domestic currency that they must sell when speculating in anticipation of a devaluation.

Chapter 8

Options for the Rest of the World

As economic and financial integration proceeds, other parts of the world will be exposed to the same pressures experienced by members of the European Union (EU). The dilemma confronting countries that are small, open, specialized, and inflation prone will be particularly stark. Although many of them have attempted in the past to peg their exchange rates, as predicted by the literature on optimum currency areas, the rise of capital mobility, the growing permeability of capital controls, and the spread of democratization will render their pegs increasingly fragile and difficult to maintain. They will then confront the choice with which the members of the EU are already faced: floating versus monetary unification.

Compared to Western Europe, the political prerequisites for monetary unification are less advanced in other parts of the world. The time required to develop them should not be exaggerated: Europe moved in two generations from open warfare to political conditions that make monetary unification conceivable. Where the starting point is more favorable, it may be possible to move more quickly. But where political conflict is as intense as it was in Western Europe fifty years ago, history cautions against anticipating early monetary unification. This observation suggests that floating exchange rates will become increasingly prevalent in other parts of the world.

If the literature on optimum currency areas is any guide, large, diversified economies like those of the United States, Japan, and Germany can afford to continue floating against one another. The very different economic conditions that prevail in the three countries imply that significant compromises of domestic economic objectives would be entailed in any effort to stabilize exchange rates among them. All the factors that render exchange rate pegs and narrow target zones problematic elsewhere would undermine attempts to peg exchange rates among the yen, deutsche mark, and dollar. Furthermore the political preconditions for an alternative as radical as monetary unification are unlikely to develop in the foreseeable future.

Assuming that exchange rates among the dollar, yen, and deutsche mark continue to fluctuate against one another, smaller countries will be confronted with the question of to which major currency they should pay special attention when framing their international monetary policies. Assuming the continued pursuit of policies of price stability in the countries issuing the three anchor currencies, capital- and commodity-market links are likely to shape their decisions. Such considerations point to the continued importance of the dollar as an anchor or reference currency in the Western Hemisphere, of the deutsche mark or ECU and the dollar in Central and Eastern Europe, and of a number of different reference currencies, including but not limited to the yen, in Asia. Less obviously these medium-term solutions may themselves set in motion a process leading to the creation of two or three regional monetary unions in the twenty-first century.

Optimum Currency Considerations

Bayoumi and Eichengreen have applied Blanchard and Quah's methodology for estimating supply and demand disturbances to data for thirty-nine countries. Cross-country correlations of these disturbances are summarized in tables 8-1 and 8-2. Shaded entries indicate significant correlations.[1]

Consider first the supply disturbances in table 8-1, on the grounds that these are least likely to change over time. The EU member states identified in chapter 7 as plausible candidates for monetary union (Germany, France, Belgium, the Netherlands, and Denmark) stand out all the more starkly when the correlation of their supply disturbances is juxtaposed against the correlations of other regions. No

1. For a discussion of how the level of statistical significance was determined, see Bayoumi and Eichengreen (forthcoming).

Table 8-1. *Correlations of Supply Disturbances across Different Geographic Regions*

	Germany	France	Netherlands	Belgium	Denmark	Austria	Switzerland	Italy	United Kingdom	Spain	Portugal	Ireland	Sweden	Norway	Finland
						Western Europe									
Germany	1.00														
France	0.52	1.00													
Netherlands	0.54	0.36	1.00												
Belgium	0.62	0.46	0.56	1.00											
Denmark	0.68	0.54	0.56	0.37	1.00										
Austria	0.41	0.28	0.38	0.47	0.49	1.00									
Switzerland	0.38	0.25	0.58	0.47	0.36	0.39	1.00								
Italy	0.21	0.28	0.39	-0.00	0.15	0.06	-0.04	1.00							
United Kingdom	0.12	0.12	0.13	0.12	-0.05	-0.25	0.16	0.28	1.00						
Spain	0.33	0.21	0.17	0.23	0.22	0.25	0.07	0.20	0.01	1.00					
Portugal	0.21	0.33	0.11	0.40	-0.04	-0.03	0.13	0.22	0.27	0.51	1.00				
Ireland	-0.00	-0.21	0.11	-0.02	-0.32	0.08	0.08	0.14	0.05	-0.15	0.01	1.00			
Sweden	0.31	0.30	0.43	0.06	0.35	0.01	0.44	0.46	0.41	0.20	0.39	0.10	1.00		
Norway	-0.27	-0.11	-0.39	-0.26	-0.37	-0.21	-0.18	0.01	0.27	-0.09	0.26	0.08	0.10	1.00	
Finland	0.22	0.12	-0.25	0.06	0.30	0.11	0.06	-0.32	-0.04	0.07	-0.13	-0.23	-0.10	-0.08	1.00

East Asia

	Japan	Taiwan	Korea	Thailand	Hong Kong	Singapore	Malaysia	Indo-nesia	Philip-pines	Australia	New Zealand
Japan	1.00										
Taiwan	0.61	1.00									
Korea	0.46	0.54	1.00								
Thailand	0.32	0.59	0.36	1.00							
Hong Kong	0.29	0.28	0.05	0.31	1.00						
Singapore	-0.10	0.25	0.02	0.29	0.63	1.00					
Malaysia	-0.02	0.06	-0.03	0.35	0.47	0.71	1.00				
Indonesia	0.14	-0.03	-0.10	0.13	0.53	0.55	0.52	1.00			
Philippines	0.10	0.37	-0.11	-0.06	0.05	0.05	-0.03	0.03	1.00		
Australia	0.12	0.21	0.19	0.14	-0.16	-0.22	0.03	0.09	0.23	1.00	
New Zealand	0.01	0.19	-0.25	0.15	-0.12	0.13	-0.11	0.01	-0.06	-0.41	1.00

Table 8-1. (continued)

The Americas

	United States	Canada	Mexico	Colombia	Venez-uela	Ecuador	Peru	Brazil	Bolivia	Paraguay	Uruguay	Argentina	Chile
United States	1.00												
Canada	-0.47	1.00											
Mexico	-0.59	0.35	1.00										
Colombia	-0.02	0.05	0.25	1.00									
Venezuela	0.09	0.34	-0.42	0.15	1.00								
Ecuador	-0.02	0.37	0.27	0.20	0.36	1.00							
Peru	-0.40	0.05	0.37	0.07	0.10	0.28	1.00						
Brazil	0.24	0.13	-0.08	0.07	0.13	0.40	0.38	1.00					
Bolivia	-0.65	0.72	0.65	0.18	0.00	0.29	0.54	0.17	1.00				
Paraguay	-0.34	0.45	0.37	0.06	0.12	-0.07	0.16	0.22	0.39	1.00			
Uruguay	0.27	-0.31	-0.26	-0.35	0.05	-0.21	0.01	-0.06	-0.20	-0.08	1.00		
Argentina	-0.30	0.08	-0.18	0.10	0.27	-0.01	0.36	0.34	0.06	0.06	-0.48	1.00	
Chile	-0.18	0.03	0.23	0.09	-0.33	-0.41	0.19	-0.23	0.17	0.21	-0.33	0.21	1.00

Source: Bayoumi and Eichengreen (forthcoming). Shaded entries indicate significant correlations.

Table 8-2. Correlations of Demand Disturbances across Different Geographic Regions

	Germany	France	Netherlands	Belgium	Denmark	Austria	Switzerland	Italy	United Kingdom	Spain	Portugal	Ireland	Sweden	Norway	Finland
						Western Europe									
Germany	1.00														
France	0.30	1.00													
Netherlands	0.21	0.34	1.00												
Belgium	0.36	0.53	0.52	1.00											
Denmark	0.34	0.32	0.20	0.30	1.00										
Austria	0.32	0.50	0.29	0.56	0.30	1.00									
Switzerland	0.18	0.42	0.37	0.28	0.22	0.45	1.00								
Italy	0.22	0.62	0.24	0.49	0.06	0.44	0.32	1.00							
United Kingdom	0.09	0.20	-0.05	-0.03	-0.00	-0.15	-0.08	0.05	1.00						
Spain	-0.10	0.53	0.11	0.26	0.25	0.30	0.04	0.43	0.23	1.00					
Portugal	0.24	0.47	0.05	0.45	0.30	0.60	0.36	0.63	0.24	0.32	1.00				
Ireland	0.06	0.09	0.39	0.00	0.34	-0.12	0.19	-0.08	0.25	0.02	-0.01	1.00			
Sweden	0.10	0.18	0.29	0.36	0.18	0.02	-0.07	0.25	0.18	-0.01	0.08	0.30	1.00		
Norway	-0.24	0.01	-0.14	-0.24	-0.11	-0.16	-0.11	-0.30	0.13	0.14	-0.19	-0.20	-0.11	1.00	
Finland	0.10	0.47	0.32	0.60	0.36	0.53	0.30	0.65	0.16	0.40	0.54	0.17	0.33	-0.21	1.00

Table 8-2. (continued)

	East Asia										
	Japan	Taiwan	Korea	Thailand	Hong Kong	Singapore	Malaysia	Indo-nesia	Philip-pines	Australia	New Zealand
Japan	1.00										
Taiwan	-0.01	1.00									
Korea	0.19	0.33	1.00								
Thailand	-0.04	0.54	0.32	1.00							
Hong Kong	0.23	0.22	0.05	0.43	1.00						
Singapore	-0.09	0.44	0.27	0.70	0.37	1.00					
Malaysia	0.12	0.41	0.43	0.58	0.54	0.67	1.00				
Indonesia	0.16	0.17	0.17	0.36	0.62	0.64	0.58	1.00			
Philippines	0.29	0.09	0.16	0.15	-0.19	-0.05	-0.11	0.04	1.00		
Australia	0.22	0.20	0.46	0.32	0.32	0.34	0.50	0.05	-0.01	1.00	
New Zealand	0.00	-0.39	-0.41	0.10	0.43	0.13	0.06	0.09	-0.06	0.21	1.00

The Americas

	United States	Canada	Mexico	Colombia	Venezuela	Ecuador	Peru	Brazil	Bolivia	Paraguay	Uruguay	Argentina	Chile
United States	1.00												
Canada	0.30	1.00											
Mexico	-0.12	0.37	1.00										
Colombia	0.07	-0.09	-0.27	1.00									
Venezuela	0.06	0.47	0.20	0.29	1.00								
Ecuador	0.19	0.28	-0.21	0.24	0.61	1.00							
Peru	0.20	0.27	0.50	-0.33	0.05	-0.09	1.00						
Brazil	0.03	0.59	0.27	0.08	0.70	0.52	0.35	1.00					
Bolivia	0.09	0.07	0.06	-0.02	-0.20	-0.19	0.18	0.02	1.00				
Paraguay	0.11	0.50	0.23	0.39	0.51	0.13	-0.04	0.38	-0.18	1.00			
Uruguay	0.35	0.04	-0.01	0.07	-0.26	-0.45	0.25	0.24	-0.13	0.08	1.00		
Argentina	0.08	0.07	0.08	-0.08	0.35	0.29	0.35	0.15	0.01	0.33	-0.41	1.00	
Chile	0.50	0.66	0.06	0.21	0.37	0.37	-0.26	0.11	0.26	0.37	-0.24	0.05	1.00

Source: Bayoumi and Eichengreen (forthcoming). Shaded entries indicate significant correlations.

other region of comparable size comes as close to satisfying this criterion for constituting an optimum currency area.[2]

In Asia two sets of significant correlations are evident: those among Japan, Taiwan, and Korea, and those among Singapore, Indonesia, and Malaysia. In the Western Hemisphere, in contrast, no country's supply disturbances are significantly correlated with those of the United States; indeed the majority of such correlations are negative despite the existence of close economic ties.

Finally note that the correlations of supply disturbances hitting the U.S., Japanese, and German economies are uniformly small and insignificant, suggesting that an attempt to stabilize the exchange rates among the dollar, deutsche mark, and yen would involve a considerable compromise of domestic economic objectives.[3]

Since the demand disturbances are dominated by monetary and fiscal policies, they are more of historical interest than a guide for future policy. There are a large number of significant positive correlations in Western Europe, but, given the variety of different international monetary regimes through which the region has passed, these show no clear pattern. The same can be said of the Western Hemisphere. Only in Asia is there evidence of a group of countries with highly correlated demand disturbances, namely Hong Kong, Singapore, Malaysia, Indonesia, and Thailand, which is similar to one of the groupings that emerges from the analysis of supply disturbances.

Options for Non-EU Europe

I start my consideration of international monetary options for diffferent parts of the world with non-EU Europe.

European Free Trade Association

Austria's participation in the EU and in any prospective European monetary union is a fait accompli; currently the country comes closer than any EU member but Luxembourg and possibly the Netherlands

2. Austria and Switzerland, neither of which is an EU member at the time of writing (although the former is certain to be in the next wave of entrants), clearly belong in this group as well.

3. Consistent with this conclusion simulations of empirically based macroeconomic models suggest that fixing exchange rates among the United States, Japan, and Germany would actually increase the variance of macroeconomic variables; see Taylor (1986); Frenkel, Goldstein, and Masson (1989); Bryant, Hooper, and Mann (1993).

to satisfying the conditions that the Maastricht Treaty sets down for participation. Other countries in the association have both political and economic obstacles to surmount. Switzerland and the Nordic countries hesitate to compromise their sovereignty because of traditions of political neutrality and social distinctiveness. Political neutrality is less of an issue with the end of the cold war, however, and distinctive socioeconomic institutions like the Swedish welfare state that would be threatened by EU membership will have to be scaled back anyway in response to rising international capital mobility and other competitive pressures. At the time of writing only Switzerland has reaffirmed its lack of interest in joining the EU; early soundings suggest that referendums on the issue have more support in Finland and Sweden than in Norway.

Even if the Nordic countries enter the EU it is not obvious that they will seek early membership in its monetary union. Asymmetric disturbances will make membership in a European monetary union especially difficult for Finland, Iceland, and Norway. These countries remain specialized in the products of the primary sector (timber, fish, and energy) and experience very different supply shocks than the more industrial economies of the EU. The collapse of Finland's Soviet trade, which was a major factor leading to the crisis that forced the country to abandon its policy of pegging the markka to the ECU in 1991–92, is only a specific illustration of the general point. The rise in Nordic unemployment, which coincided with the pursuit of policies pegging the currency to the ECU or the deutsche mark—policies that ultimately had to be abandoned under duress—has left the citizens of the Nordic countries deeply skeptical about the desirability of exchange rate pegging, much less monetary unification.

If the Nordic countries are not in the first wave of participants in the European monetary union, as seems likely, their currencies will continue to float without an explicit exchange rate target, much as they do today. The question will then become whether swings in their exchange rates will create trade imbalances and political pressures that will strain these countries' relations with other participants in the Single Market.

Eastern Europe

With the end of central planning, the transition economies of Eastern Europe moved quickly to eliminate restrictions on current account convertibility while maintaining controls on capital account transactions. They adopted a variety of different exchange rate arrangements. Czechoslovakia pegged its rate. Poland adopted a fixed peg against the U.S. dollar in 1990, shifting in October 1991 to a crawling basket peg with a preannounced schedule of daily adjustments. Hungary has used an adjustable crawling peg, under which the exchange rate can be changed unexpectedly. Bulgaria and more recently Romania have allowed their currencies to float. Although the Bulgarian float has been relatively free of central bank intervention in the foreign exchange market, Romania managed the exchange rate heavily once it was unified in November 1991. Slovenia's central bank has gradually relaxed exchange restrictions and intervened periodically in the market for the tolar.[4]

The very different exchange arrangements adopted by the Baltic states point up the contrasting choices of the transition economies. Estonia, Latvia, and Lithuania all left the ruble zone in 1992 and created separate currencies. Estonia moved quickly to establish current account convertibility, pegging its exchange rate to the deutsche mark under a currency board system.[5] Controls on capital account transactions have been retained, a decision that, according to the argument of previous chapters, reduces the fragility of the peg.[6] Latvia also moved quickly to establish convertibility but allowed its currency to float against other convertible currencies and the Russian ruble. Although the exchange rate was officially said to float freely observers inferred that extensive central bank intervention in the foreign exchange market actually took place.[7]

This history suggests that a variety of different exchange arrangements are in principle compatible with the transition to the market. The advantage of a rigid peg like that of Estonia lies in providing a nominal anchor useful for buttressing stabilization, as described in chapter 2. The advantage of a float, whether relatively free as in Bulgaria and Slovenia or more heavily managed as in Romania, is that the exchange rate can be adjusted in response to changing balance-of-payments conditions. Both imperatives are pressing in Eastern Eu-

4. For details see Mencinger (1993); Borensztein and Masson (1993).
5. See chapter 5. Lithuania, after an extended period of high inflation, followed Estonia in establishing a currency board on April 1, 1994.
6. See Bennett (1993).
7. The official account was given in Repse (1993). Lainela and Sutela (1993) were among the observers who thought otherwise.

rope, where stabilizations are fragile and balances of payments are dislocated by economic transformation. Borensztein and Masson argue that stabilization must first be completed before other forms of adjustment can follow, but that once stabilization is locked in the nominal anchor function of a pegged rate becomes less important; this is an argument for emulating Poland's strategy of first pegging the exchange rate to maximize credibility but subsequently introducing greater flexibility to accommodate changing balance-of-payments conditions.[8] Insofar as controls on capital account transactions will be removed as these economies are integrated into the international financial system, this approach will render pegged rates, even if buttressed by currency board arrangements, more difficult to sustain.

These factors will encourage East European countries to gravitate over time toward greater exchange rate flexibility. Working in the other direction will be their desire for admission to the EU. Pegging to the deutsche mark, à la Estonia, is a way to signal the sincerity of their intent. Once the removal of capital controls renders pegging difficult, these countries may instead choose to shadow the deutsche mark without declaring a central rate or a band. If post-EMU Europe turns inward and throws up barriers against all but its immediate neighbors to the east, as Mundell predicts, this action will encourage the rest of Eastern Europe and much of the former-Soviet Union to contemplate dollar-based currency board arrangements or a Canadian-style policy of loosely shadowing the U.S. dollar.[9]

The Former Soviet Union

The situation in the former Soviet Union is of a different sort. A high degree of openness and extensive intrarepublican trade seemingly provide an economic rationale for a single currency for Russia and other former Soviet republics. Many republics share the characteristics of market economies that have traditionally pegged their currencies to that of a major trading partner (small size, sectoral specialization, underdeveloped financial markets). Many of these new nations have yet to establish well functioning, independent central

8. See Borensztein and Masson (1993).
9. See Mundell (1993).

banks, providing yet another rationale for delegating monetary functions to an outside authority.

Factors such as these provided some justification for attempting in 1991–92 to hold together the ruble zone, a monetary union in which former Soviet republics used the Russian ruble as a means of payment, unit of account, and store of value. The ruble zone nonetheless disintegrated in 1992–93, as one republic after another, starting with the Baltics and followed by Ukraine, issued coupons and currencies to supplement and replace the ruble. High inflation in Russia, fueled by monetization of the budget deficit and interenterprise debts, implied high inflation for republics using the ruble. Any argument for the ruble zone as a means of minimizing transaction costs was vitiated by hyperinflation; republics seeking to stabilize had an incentive to leave the currency area.

Meanwhile Russia had its own reasons for terminating the ruble zone.[10] As long as other republics could create rubles, set interest rates on central bank credit, and determine reserve requirements on commercial bank deposit liabilities, a free rider problem arose that greatly complicated efforts at taming Russian inflation.[11] Although only the Central Bank of Russia could print ruble banknotes, newly created central banks in other republics could extend credit to their governments and domestic enterprises by creating "bank" or "credit" rubles existing only on their balance sheets, by drawing on credit lines with the Central Bank of Russia, and by issuing coupons. In effect each republic could add to the money supply; since the resulting inflation spilled over to the entire currency union, each issuing authority had an incentive to increase its share of seigniorage revenues while exporting inflation to other ruble zone members.[12] The result was an inevitable bias toward inflation.

Solutions to this problem are to dissolve the ruble zone or to centralize control of the fiscal and financial policies of the participat-

10. The Central Bank of Russia's decision to withdraw all pre-1993 banknotes from circulation can be seen as an effort to force the issue.

11. This problem was identified early on by Buiter and Eaton (1983) and Casella and Feinstein (1989). It is explored further by Miller (1993).

12. The details are more complicated than this, since some sellers of commodities hesitate to accept a republic's bank rubles on the grounds that they may not be accepted in other republics. Bank rubles issued in republics other than Russia consequently trade at discounts to paper rubles. But this fact does not ameliorate the free rider problem created by decentralized issuance.

ing republics. Thus in October 1992 the Central Bank of Russia announced that it would no longer automatically redeem noncash rubles accumulated by Russian enterprises that originated in other republics. Countries like Ukraine that relied heavily on trade with Russia had to begin guaranteeing their own emissions, a policy tantamount to issuing a separate national currency. Ukraine formally left the ruble zone by revoking the Russian ruble's legal tender status one month later. In 1993 the Russian government demanded that other republics like Moldova that had not yet done so issue their own currencies or else deposit their gold and hard currency reserves with the Central Bank of Russia and agree to follow financial and monetary policies ordained by Moscow.

Given that it is still seeking to establish its authority over breakaway regions within the Russian republic, Moscow will surely hesitate to give other republics a voice in the formulation of policy by the Central Bank of Russia for fear that regions within the Russian Federation will demand the same voice. Remaining in the ruble zone on these terms represents a clear compromise of sovereignty, which will give pause to most former Soviet republics, given popular resentment of Moscow's hegemony. Even where economic conditions encourage currency unification, therefore, political considerations will lead to a proliferation of national currencies.[13]

The exceptions are republics with especially severe economic and political problems, such as Belarus and Tajikistan. They may be willing to sacrifice political prerogatives, including the maintenance of a separate currency and much of their fiscal and financial autonomy, in return for the foreign aid that they desperately require. The national defense argument for a separate currency as a revenue source of last resort is least compelling for republics that cannot realistically hope to defend their borders against a much larger neighbor. As Luxembourg does with Belgium, they may prefer to delegate control over their monetary affairs.

Belarus has gone the furthest in this direction.[14] It is a small country of eleven million people whose gross domestic production is

13. Thus Kazakhstan and Uzbekistan signed a multilateral agreement with Russia on September 7, 1993, committing to participate in a currency union and to pursue unified monetary and fiscal policies. Once Russia made clear that it would demand that they deposit all gold and hard currency reserves with the Central Bank of Russia, the two countries terminated negotiations and introduced their own currencies.

14. In fact there remains considerable internal dissent from this policy, most notably on the part of Belarus's central bank, for which monetary union would mean dissolution.

barely 5 percent of Russia's; 70 percent of Belarus's imports, including 90 percent of its energy, come from Russia. As a producer of little energy it is dependent on subsidized oil imports. In 1993–94 inflation in Belarus exceeded even that in Russia; as of April 1994 the zaichik traded at more than ten to the ruble.[15] On April 12, 1994, the prime ministers of Russia and Belarus signed a monetary union treaty, in which Belarus agreed to hand over control of monetary and credit policies to the Central Bank of Russia. Russia is to get a free lease on military bases for its troops, while Belarus will enjoy cheaper Russian oil and gas as a result of the lifting of all customs and tariff duties and the removal of transit fees.

The vast majority of former Soviet republics aspire to defend their borders and control their fiscal and financial destinies; they will therefore maintain national currencies.[16] Thus Kazakhstan and Uzbekistan, which agreed in August 1992 to harmonize their tax and customs rates with Russia's, limit the provision of credit to enterprise, and delegate their monetary policies to Moscow in order to remain in the ruble zone, opted subsequently to issue national monies. For them the question becomes how to manage their exchange rates. As long as such countries limit and control capital account transactions as part of their strategy for completing the transition to the market, pegging will remain feasible, especially where supported by the creation of a currency board. Once liberalization extends to capital account transactions, however, they will be confronted with the familiar dilemma of whether to float or to resume discussions about the establishment of a monetary union.

Africa

Like Eastern Europe and the former Soviet Union, Africa is characterized by a wide variety of international monetary arrangements, ranging from inconvertibility, dual exchange rates, and regional clearinghouses on the one hand to convertibility and monetary union on the other.[17] Many African countries peg to another currency (the

15. Details in the remainder of this paragraph are drawn from Erlanger (1994).

16. Another Belarus-like counterexample is Tajikistan, a central Asian republic that uses the Russian ruble and receives two-thirds of its state budget from Russia in return for providing Russia with bases from which to fight an Islamic insurgency supported from Afganistan.

17. Space limitations prevent a thorough analysis of these arrangements. For details see Hugon, Cerruti, and Collignon (1992).

French franc, the U.S. dollar, the South African rand, or the SDR (Special Drawing Rights); usually these pegs are supported by restrictions on capital account transactions.[18] Once they relax capital controls the states of this region, like other developing countries, will then be faced with the decision of whether to introduce more flexibility into their currency links (as Sierra Leone, Zambia, Burundi, Guinea, and Guinea-Bissau have already done) or to foreswear monetary autonomy in the manner of the members of the CFA franc zone.

That Africa already features two full-fledged monetary unions suggests that this latter choice, whether achieved through replication or expansion, is not impossible. But the special circumstances that have sustained the Central African Monetary Union (CAMU) and the West African Monetary Union (WAMU) since the 1960s raise doubts about feasibility elsewhere. CAMU and WAMU both grew out of the financial arrangements used by France to administer her colonies.[19] Prior to gaining their independence France's African colonies used CFA francs, convertible at the rate of 0.5 CFA franc per French franc. In the 1970s they formed a pair of monetary unions, each with a central bank issuing a single currency. The exchange rate between the currencies of the CFA franc zone (since the mid-1970s, the franc de la Communauté Financière d'Afrique and the franc de la Cooperation Financière en Afrique Centrale) and the French franc were fixed for more than forty years.[20] In January 1994, in response to a series of adverse commodity-price shocks and a severe problem of real overvaluation (exacerbated by the French government's policy of keeping the franc high relative to the currencies of other industrial countries), the currencies of the CFA franc zone were devalued.[21] Significantly, despite disagreements among the participating African

18. Franc peggers include not only members of the CFA franc (francs des Colonies Françaises d'Afrique) zone; Comoros has an independent currency that is pegged to the franc. The prominent exception to this statement about the prevalence of capital controls is the CFA franc countries, which, while maintaining some restrictions on capital account transactions, are quite open to financial flows.

19. For additional details on matters discussed in the following paragraphs see Boughton (1992).

20. The Central Bank of the Comoros, which issues its own currency, the Comorian franc, also maintains a fixed rate against the French franc and is a member of the franc zone.

21. The terms of trade of the franc zone as a whole deteriorated by almost 45 percent between 1985 and 1993.

states over the magnitude and very desirability of the devaluation, this event did not disrupt the operation of the two monetary unions.

What holds together the two African monetary unions and sustains their pegs to the French franc? Simply put, the stability of the exchange rate against the French franc is underwritten by the French treasury. France provides unlimited support to maintain the convertibility of the CFA franc at par, purchasing however many CFA francs it has to in order to keep the price from falling. That France retains a sense of responsibility for its former colonies in West Africa reconciles it to the expenditure of resources that these operations entail, while the large size of its economy relative to that of West Africa makes the burden manageable. In addition the procedures followed by the two West African central banks serve to reassure the French government that its intervention obligations will not grow without limit. When a deficit of a CFA franc country results in a drop in the operations account of one of the West African central banks at the French treasury, the central bank responds by raising its rediscount rates for the country concerned and restricting the availability of rediscounting facilities. The French government is able to monitor the actions of the African countries through an agreement that gives French officials seats on the boards of their two central banks.[22]

What lends credibility to two central banks' promise to respond in this way? For one thing failing to raise rediscount rates and restrict credit might ultimately threaten the franc zone countries' access to credit in Paris. In addition the agreement between the CFA franc countries and the French treasury requires the former to deposit 65 percent of their international reserves with the French treasury, resources that would be placed at risk in the event of a dispute. Finally the fact that France is the principal source of foreign aid to these countries provides an additional lever.

This arrangement has delivered a remarkable record of price stability: inflation in the CFA franc zone has roughly matched French inflation (in the low single digits), in contrast to the much higher inflation rates of neighboring African countries. Exchange rate stability has promoted trade within the zone and between West Africa and France. The question is whether inability to use the exchange rate as an instrument of adjustment has at the same time had real economic costs. The participating countries experience very different terms of

---

22. For details see Boughton (1993).

trade shocks, since some specialize in the production and export of minerals, others in agricultural products, and still others in petroleum. Labor mobility across participating countries is only moderate. All this suggests that inability to adjust the exchange rate in response to shocks has had economic costs. Devarajan and Rodrick conclude that the CFA franc countries would have been better off had they forsaken monetary union for exchange rate flexibility and policy autonomy. They would have enjoyed a superior capacity to adjust.[23] This conclusion is predicated, of course, on the assumption that the exchange rate would have been used sensibly rather than being misused by the authorities. The negative experience of other African countries suggests caution in recommending that they move to the other extreme.

What is the scope for expanding these arrangements? Virtually all the countries participating in the two African monetary unions are former French colonies that receive preferential treatment by the French treasury. Other parts of Africa could not automatically expect to receive comparable privileges. Nor would countries without a history of French colonial ties be as inclined to accept French officials on their central bank boards. Yet insofar as the CFA franc zone represents a region of monetary stability, other African countries without such ties may wish to join. That Equatorial Guinea, a small country contiguous to the CAMU countries but without colonial or close economic ties to France, did so in 1985 confirms that this suggestion is not merely a hypothetical one.

Countries not in a position to join one of the two existing African monetary unions will face the familiar dilemma of whether to attempt to maintain restrictions on capital account transactions and perhaps experiment with a currency board arrangement, or else to manage their floating rates, presumably by shadowing one of the three major currencies. Mundell suggests that, notwithstanding their colonial links to Europe, African countries outside the CFA zone are likely to build such arrangements on the dollar.[24]

The Western Hemisphere

The currencies of Canada and Mexico continue to float against the U.S. dollar (Mexico's within a band), notwithstanding the dramatic

23. See Devarajan and Rodrick (1991).
24. See Mundell (1993).

steps underway to create a North American free trade area. If West European integration intensifies the dislocations caused by exchange rate swings and therefore requires a single currency to support a truly integrated market, is the same not true of the United States, Canada, and Mexico? Why, in other words, have North American Free Trade Agreement (NAFTA) negotiations not given rise to pressure for exchange rate stabilization, which, according to the logic of this book, will lead in turn to monetary union?

One answer is that they have. Devaluations of the peso that reduced Mexican relative to U.S. labor costs in the 1980s figured prominently in U.S. labor's campaign against the NAFTA treaty's ratification. Conscious of this danger, on April 26, 1994, the United States, Mexico, and Canada announced the creation of a multi-billion-dollar fund to finance intervention in support of the Mexican peso and to protect the peso against "onslaughts by global speculators."[25]

For the time being the tensions caused in the United States by exchange rate swings are attenuated by the small size of the Mexican economy relative to that of the United States.[26] As long as Mexico's economy is only 5 percent the size of that of the United States, the dislocations caused by a change in the peso-dollar rate will be small compared to those experienced by Germany when its exchange rate changes vis-à-vis France. In addition, economic integration caused by NAFTA will remain limited for some time: many of NAFTA's scheduled reductions in tariffs and barriers to foreign investment will be phased in gradually over the next ten to fifteen years.

One can imagine that the pressure for exchange rate stabilization will grow. An exchange rate swing that reduced Mexican minimum wages in dollars by 10 or 20 percent would do much to fan U.S. labor's opposition to intra–North American liberalization. The Mexican government recently announced that the Mexican minimum wage would be raised in line with labor productivity, in order to reassure U.S. labor worried about the loss of jobs in labor-intensive sectors resulting from exchange-rate swings.

If, with the removal of remaining capital controls, pegging the peso to the dollar grows increasingly problematic, the Mexican government will find itself in an increasingly difficult position. Monetary

25. Friedman (1994, pp. D1, D18).
26. This and many of the arguments that follow apply also to Canada, although in this discussion I focus on the Mexican case.

union with the United States would have to overcome U.S. opposition to making Mexico a Federal Reserve district and the great weight Mexico attaches to its sovereignty, monetary and otherwise. Such a scenario is not a short-term possibility: in Europe, forty years of economic integration have not sufficed to produce an analogous outcome. A currency board arrangement à la Argentina is conceivable, although it will prove increasingly difficult to sustain once democratization introduces the prospect of significant changes in the composition of the government. There may be no practical alternative but to emulate Canada by allowing the currency rate to float subject to central bank management, in the hope that the market pressures preventing the Mexican central bank from holding the rate within an explicit band do not imply exchange rate fluctuations on an order that antagonize powerful lobbies in its trading partner to the north.

Other Latin American countries face similar options. Chile and Argentina both peg to the dollar (the former less rigidly than the latter); both aspire to gain NAFTA membership. Other Latin American nations will follow. Countries with recent histories of high inflation, most prominently Brazil, are likely to experiment with Argentine-style currency board solutions, whereas others may choose the Chilean option of a wide, permissive target zone. Insofar as these countries, compared to Mexico, are further away geographically from and trade less heavily with the United States, pressure to stabilize the exchange rate as a condition for market access should be correspondingly less intense.

In the long term it is at least conceivable that a Latin American monetary union could grow out of a regional trade arrangement like Mercosur (the prospective free trade area for portions of South America). Countries such as Argentina, which have stabilized, complain loudly about exchange dumping and unfair import competition from countries that have not. Once again, for political economy reasons it may only be possible to bring to fruition a regional free trade arrangement like Mercosur if this source of political and economic conflict is eliminated. Countries like Brazil with persistent inflation problems could conceivably regard a regional monetary union hooked to a regional free trade agreement as a way of credibly committing to the pursuit of policies of price stability. But their neighbors like Argentina find it more attractive to look northward to free trade with the United States, and they attach higher priority to a stable dollar link than to a monetary union with a Brazil, whose resiliency in the face of inflation is likely to remain inferior to their own currency board solution.

Thus whatever momentum develops for a Latin American monetary union will be undercut by the desire for closer trade relations with the United States and therefore for a dollar link.

Asia

In Asia regional integration has been proceeding more slowly than in other parts of the world, reflecting historically based tensions between Japan and the other countries along with the absence of an institutional initiative like the EU to smooth them over. The Association of South East Asian Nations (ASEAN) has endorsed the creation of an ASEAN free trade association, but little progress has occurred to date. Although the share of Pacific Asian countries' trade that remains within the region rose from 20 to nearly 30 percent between 1980 and 1990, most of the increase reflected income growth and proximity rather than policies designed to promote trade within the region. And 30 percent is still a low number by the standards of, say, the EU. Intraregional financial links are of increasing importance. Other Asian countries account for 41 percent of all direct foreign investment in Indonesia, 72 percent in Malaysia, 60 percent in the Philippines, and 69 percent in Thailand.[27]

Working in the other direction is an unusual degree of labor mobility in East Asia, mainly from the less-developed ASEAN nations to more industrialized, capital-abundant newly industrialized countries.[28] Singapore, which receives foreign workers from neighboring Malaysia, Indonesia, the Philippines, and Thailand, has a larger share of foreigners in its labor force than any industrialized country aside from Switzerland. In 1987 emigration from the Philippines accounted for fully 2 percent of the labor force. This level of labor mobility, if allowed to persist, would ease adjustment to asymmetric shocks in the absence of exchange rate changes.

Intra-Asian trade and financial links are certain to grow, but trade and investment links with the United States will also remain important, raising the question of whether currencies in the region should

27. See Goto and Hamada (1993, p. 34).
28. See Goto and Hamada (1992).

follow the yen or the dollar. Hong Kong has used a currency board scheme to peg to the U.S. dollar. But most countries in the region allow their currencies to float, reflecting the dual importance of the U.S. and Japanese markets. Frankel and Wei find that the currencies of Thailand, Korea, and China tend to follow the dollar quite closely, the other East Asian currencies less so. Only for Singapore is there a statistically significant role for the yen in local exchange rate determination.[29]

Basket pegs have been used by Thailand and, for certain periods, other East Asian countries, but rigid versions will become increasingly difficult to support with the relaxation of the region's traditionally stringent capital controls. As elsewhere the choices will be floating versus monetary unification. Other than Hong Kong and Singapore, the countries of this region do not possess the sort of small economies for which a distinct national currency imposes insuperable costs. For this reason and because of slow progress in building the relevant international institutions, floating is likely to remain more attractive than monetary unification in the medium term.

---

29. See Frankel and Wei (1993). At the same time there is considerable coherence in fluctuations in national money supply growth rates in the region. Goto and Hamada (1993) report a principal components analysis for eight east Asian countries, excluding Japan, and find that the first principal component explains 52 percent of the variation in money growth rates across countries, a finding that exceeds comparable measures for the large EC countries.

Chapter 9

Conclusion

A S the middle ground of pegged but adjustable exchange rates and exchange rate target zones is hollowed out and policymakers are confronted with a choice between floating and monetary unification, large and small countries in different political circumstances will respond in different ways. Large, well-diversified economies like those of the United States, Japan, and Germany face the lowest costs of continuing to float against one another.[1] The political preconditions for monetary unification between them remain remote. They may continue to mouth platitudes about the desirability of macroeconomic policy coordination and exchange rate stabilization, but ultimately they will hesitate to sacrifice domestic economic objectives in the interest of stabilizing international currency values. They will hesitate to establish international institutions with teeth sufficiently sharp to force significant adaptations of domestic economic policies. They lack a web of interlocking political agreements like those that the European Union has developed over two generations to make significant compromises of sovereignty conceivable.

Smaller countries will find it more costly to float against one another, as the theory of optimum currency areas suggests. Some such countries may opt for monetary union with the relevant partner or partners. This response is most likely in Western Europe, where the political preconditions are relatively well developed, although even there the movement toward monetary union is by no means a fait accompli. Even in Europe it remains to be seen

1. One may want to add Russia to this list once stabilization and liberalization are complete and steady growth resumes.

134

whether the political commonality of interest exists to establish an institution for the management of a single currency for a number of like-sized countries.

Still smaller countries will find it attractive to hitch their currencies to that of a larger neighbor, forsaking their monetary autonomy. They may seek to do so informally, as does the Netherlands with Germany (in the sense that it holds its currency within an even narrower band against the deutsche mark than is required by the ERM), or formally, as under the currency board arrangements of Argentina (which pegs to the dollar) and Estonia (which pegs to the deutsche mark). Whether they will succeed for any period of time in pegging their currencies to that of a larger neighbor is another question. As argued in this book, changes in technology, market structure, and politics will work against them. The institutionalized structure of labor markets will restrict the responsiveness of their prices and wages. The increasingly politicized environment in which monetary policy is made will erode the credibility of governments' commitment to exchange rate rules. Changes in technology will increase international capital mobility, limiting the capacity of governments to contain market pressures at an acceptable political cost. Together these changes will undermine the viability of monetary rules under which governments commit to pegging their currencies, whether in the context of a pegged but adjustable rate scheme or in the context of a target zone, and under either a central bank operating procedure or a parliamentary statute.

Whether such countries adopt currency board arrangements or, more likely, attempt to shadow a major currency at a distance, they will face the issue of which currency to follow. In Eastern Europe this will be the deutsche mark or its successor, unless the European Union turns into a Fortress Europe, restricting access to its market for all but the first tier of East European countries and encouraging others to link their fortunes to the more open U.S. market by tying their currencies to the dollar. However European trade politics develop, a dollar link is the most plausible option in the Western Hemisphere.

One can imagine that these arrangements, in conjunction with the expansion of regional trade initiatives, could evolve into larger monetary unions in both Europe and the Western Hemisphere in the distant future. In East Asia and the former Soviet Union, in contrast, the economic interests of countries are more varied, and the legacy of political enmity remains more intense. There, it seems likely, a wide variety of exchange arrangements will continue to prevail.

Is there a possibility that such regional arrangements might eventually evolve into a single currency for the world, as Cooper and Bergsten have suggested?[2] A case for this outcome can be made if one subscribes to the premise that deep economic integration renders policy rules based on explicit exchange rate targets—such as pegged but adjustable rates, crawling pegs, and target zones–problematic. As commodity, labor and financial integration proceeds, floating will grow progressively less attractive. Yet the constraints on the emergence of a single world currency are not merely economic; they are political. They require political integration sufficient to support a system of global fiscal transfers (global fiscal federalism) and to render the governance of a global central bank politically feasible. Even in the aftermath of the cold war, the political preconditions for a single world currency remain very far away.

2. See Cooper (1990) and Bergsten (1993).

Comments

Alberto Giovannini

Barry Eichengreen's volume is a clear exposition of the current issues in international monetary policy and their implications for the evolution of international monetary arrangements. The author devotes considerable space to setting the terminology as well as the record straight. Unilateral and multilateral monetary regimes are reviewed. The accumulated wisdom on recent monetary history as well as on the very recent international monetary turbulence is concisely described.

The question posed by the book, as it appears in the title, is a mixture of positive and normative economics: which exchange rate regimes will be adopted? Which regimes should be adopted? Eichengreen's answer seems to make the normative and the positive coincide. Countries will choose what is best for them, and as he has shown, the best arrangements are quite different from country to country.

Two general points are made. The first is that the evolution of world capital markets is such that the options available to national governments will be fewer. Increasingly the choice for a country will be either to float its currency or to join a currency union. The second point is that the likelihood of a worldwide currency, as predicted and advocated by some influential observers, is very slim. The reason is that in a world of fiat currencies the institutional reforms needed to support such an arrangement are daunting and difficult to implement politically.

Alberto Giovannini is Jerome A. Chazen Professor of International Business, Columbia University, research fellow at the Centre for Economic Policy Research, and research associate of the National Bureau of Economic Research.

In the next section I reconsider some aspects of Eichengreen's method and ask to what extent we can make statements about the way in which the world monetary system will or should evolve. In the concluding section, I draw implications from that discussion.

Economic and Political Determinants of Exchange Rate Regimes

In discussing what determines exchange rate regimes, Eichengreen starts appropriately from the accepted view: exchange rates are determined in asset markets and, left to themselves, display a volatility that is characteristic of many asset prices. However, unlike many asset prices, fluctuations in exchange rates are often a source of great concern for governments and central banks.

A common device to limit exchange rate fluctuations is "fixing" exchange rates, that is, allowing exchange rates to fluctuate within specified bands.[1] Eichengreen's point is that, because of increased international capital market integration, pegging the exchange rate will become, if it is not already, an impractical solution.

One of the novelties in the revival of the literature on international monetary arrangements of the 1980s and 1990s is the general skepticism toward pegged exchange rates. Applications of rational-expectations reasoning have prompted several of us to claim that pegged exchange rates are vulnerable to credibility problems and ultimately to self-fulfilling speculative attacks, and that they are not really defensible in open international capital markets, characterized by flows of short-term money that overwhelm the capacity of central banks' isolated or concerted intervention. I am in general sympathetic with an approach that emphasizes the potential instabilities of foreign exchange markets, and indeed I have been applying these ideas in my own discussion of the project of monetary union in Europe. (In particular in the case of Europe I have claimed that the only stable regimes are either a monetary union or flexible exchange rates.[2])

Eichengreen seems to have pushed these observations to the extreme, both here and in his related work with Charles Wyplosz. There

1. Incidentally, I find Eichengreen's detailed taxonomy a little bit redundant. All exchange rate regimes can be subsumed under three main arrangements: flexible, managed floating, and pegged exchange rates, with a given band width.

2. See Giovannini (1991).

he claims that the vulnerability of pegged exchange rates to non-fundamental speculative attacks can justify the adoption of some form of international capital controls.

The foreign exchange turbulence of recent years should certainly provide important evidence to evaluate the polarization view of international monetary regimes offered by Eichengreen. Countries that peg their exchange rates, either unilaterally or with the financial safeguards provided by multilateral arrangements, incur some costs and obtain some benefits. The costs are summarized by the potential for ex-post interest rate differentials, which grow larger as the credibility problems of the exchange rate peg increase. The benefits are the minimization of real exchange rate volatility as well as the general benefits associated with the slow build-up of credibility.

The calculus of costs and benefits of exchange rate pegging does not yield unambiguous answers. Thus the extreme polarization view put forward by Eichengreen should be reconsidered. Several countries still find exchange rate pegging a practical and desirable regime, even if it entails parity adjustments from time to time. Indeed, the experience of the past year suggests that, for example, the imposition of capital controls in France would have proved damaging: the country survived a number of periods of turbulence in exchange rates while maintaining long-term interest rates within a very acceptable range over Germany's. Current yields on ten-year government bonds are in France only fifty basis points above those of the same bonds in Germany,[3] and the differential has been even narrower over the past year. To conclude, while pegged exchange rates are certainly a less stable regime than floating rates and, by definition, a currency union, it is probably too early to declare their (current or future) demise.

I now turn to another difficulty in the exercise of predicting or suggesting exchange rate regimes for the twenty-first century: the identification of the political determinants of such regimes. The almost cyclical alternation of fixed and floating exchange rates, highlighted by the generalized reversal of exchange rate policies in Europe after the 1992 and 1993 crises, prompts two observations:

—As Eichengreen also notes, institutional design is a major hurdle to the degree of monetary coordination that is required to sustain either a regime of credibly pegged exchange rates or a monetary

3. Close of July 18, 1994. Source: Goldman Sachs International.

union. The Articles of Agreement of the International Monetary Fund, aimed at establishing international rules in a regime of fiat currencies, were not able to substitute effectively for the strict convertibility rules that characterized the classical gold standard. The provisions on parity realignments were substantially weakened and the scarce currency clause did not mention the fundamental problem that may make it arise: lack of coordination of monetary policies.[4] More recently, the EMS rules, which in principle provide for unlimited bilateral credit facilities involving currencies whose parity has reached a margin of fluctuation, were ignored by member countries during the 1992 foreign exchange crisis. Hence the fragility of institutional backup to international monetary policy coordination does explain in part this cyclical nature of international monetary arrangements.

—The alternation of different exchange rate regimes often seems to be guided by intellectual fads, rather than by a meaningful political debate within individual countries. For example in many European countries we currently hear influential opinions claiming that the idea of returning to the EMS on a large scale, or of restarting the project of monetary union, is "politically dead." The claims are made without any attempt to relate the economic effects of these exchange rate regimes to the political debate in Europe.

I have analyzed in detail the political aspects of optimum currency areas and, unlike Eichengreen, I have put forth a rather strong proposition: the political economy of alternative international monetary regimes is much fuzzier than the political economy of alternative international trade regimes.[5] In other words international trade models tell us in a rather unambiguous way which classes of voters stand to gain and which classes stand to lose from a given reform in international trade. By contrast monetary models provide us with little guidance in identifying gainers and losers in international monetary reforms. The implication is that there are no stable political constituencies for or against international monetary reform. As a result the political debate on international monetary reform is often held hostage to extraneous factors, with at best tenuous and often insignificant links with the underlying economic effects of such reforms.

4. See Giovannini (1993).
5. See Giovannini (1992).

Concluding Observations

Monetary economics cannot be claimed to be that much less precise a science than other branches of economics. However, although monetary economics helps clarify most issues surrounding the choice of international monetary regime (and recent research has added admirably to the debate), it fails to provide the final answer on questions of the magnitude that the title of this volume suggests. One of the reasons for this indeterminacy is suggested in this comment: there are no stable constituencies for or against alternative international monetary arrangements.

My other observation on Eichengreen's theses is that, despite the increased aggressiveness of agents in international financial markets, the option of pegging the exchange rate, even in a regime of free capital movements, is not one that should be discarded a priori.

The implication of my two observations is that Professor Eichengreen was, in this volume, called to an impossible task. He has, however, provided us with a set of observations of exemplary clarity, which do help us identify potential developments in the international monetary system in the twenty-first century.

Toyoo Gyohten

As the turn of the century draws nearer, there seems to be renewed interest in international monetary arrangements for the twenty-first century. There are good reasons for this revival of interest.

With the cold war behind us, many of us harbor the aspiration to create a truly global economic order. For the first time since the end of World War II virtually all countries on the globe have pledged their faith in democracy and the market economy. International economic organizations, such as the International Monetary Fund (IMF), the World Bank, and General Agreement on Tariffs and Trade enjoy nearly universal membership. The time seems ripe to establish the framework for a monetary arrangement that can support the harmonious functioning and development of the world economy.

There is also concern, particularly among the countries of the Organization for Economic Cooperation and Development (OECD), that the poor performance of their economies in terms of growth, trade, inflation, and employment may be at least partly attributable to the lack of a stable international monetary arrangement since the collapse of the Bretton Woods regime in the early 1970s. Adding to this concern are fears that exorbitant volatility and chronic misalignment of exchange rates can hurt investment and trade and also encourage protectionism.

Professor Eichengreen's volume is a great contribution to the current debate. It presents one of the most comprehensive and detailed analyses of the various arrangements conceived for the purpose of improving the performance of exchange rates. I would offer the following four comments:

—Although his survey and analysis are thorough I regret that he focuses too much on regional and subregional currency arrangements and not enough on global arrangements. We initiated the project because we were concerned about the stability of the global currency situation, which is essential to fostering economic development and political stability. What I would have hoped to hear from Professor Eichengreen were suggestions on how to improve the relationship among major international currencies—a goal that he dismisses too quickly as impossible. Discussions on monetary unions in such areas as Africa, eastern Europe, and Latin America, no matter how interest-

Toyoo Gyohten is chairman of the board of directors of the Bank of Tokyo, Ltd.

ing from an academic point of view, do not seem relevant to the questions of global currency stability.

—When we consider international monetary arrangements we should not forget the importance of the balance of power among different major currency countries. As we have learned from past experiences, stability of international monetary arrangements is best achieved when there is either a hegemonic center of power or an adequate balance of power. Professor Eichengreen does not seem to pay enough attention to this point.

—In today's huge, globalized, and liquid currency market it is quite possible that investors with large resources and a determination to seek a quick profit can play a decisive role in deciding the direction of the market. We should not underestimate their influence. Quite often these investors (or speculators) are criticized for their destabilizing influence. However, we must understand that speculators can be powerful only when they are following correctly the underlying trend of economic fundamentals. George Soros's success in the fall of 1993 and his failure in the spring of 1994 provide good proof of this assertion.

—Overshooting of exchange rates takes place when each one of a majority of market players wishfully believes that he is smart enough to become the last winner in the game even though he knows that the market is already overheated and that a reversal can happen at any moment. Under such circumstances a decisive and powerful action by the authorities can be quite effective in turning around the market. In addition, prolonged misalignment of exchange rates takes place when the market is comfortably confident that the authorities are ignorant of the fundamental disequilibrium, or that they are unable or unwilling to correct it. Under such circumstances a clear shift in macroeconomic policy is the only cure.

Two oil crises in the 1970s, the universal trend toward financial deregulation (which was prompted by the rapid expansion of the Euromoney market), and the enormous technological progress made in data processing and communication have combined to create a huge, liquid, and global financial market. The torrent of financial flows inundated the market and, in most cases national monetary authorities were helpless, even though they tried hard to control the flow and stabilize exchange rates. Their experiences disheartened the authorities, but at the same time they intensified the longing for a stable international monetary arrangement. Many of us reminisce about the heyday of the gold standard and the Bretton Woods regime; we wonder what were the conditions that supported those arrangements, whether it would be possible to restore them, and, if not, what alternatives are available to us in the twenty-first century. Under the circumstances, the theme of Eichengreen's highly motivated work is quite appropriate.

When discussing international monetary arrangements, it is important to recognize that any international monetary arrangement has two major components. One is the role of the key international currency, i.e., the decision as to which currency or asset functions as an international instrument of reserve and settlement. The second component is the arrangement under which exchange rates are designed to move. Under the gold standard gold was used as the key international instrument of reserve and settlement. The value of a given national currency unit was expressed in terms of the weight of gold. In other words, the exchange rate was fixed. The Bretton Woods regime introduced a major relaxation of this rigid system. The U.S. dollar, a national currency, was expected to play the role of the key international currency for reserve and settlement. Yet the value of the dollar was guaranteed by the U.S. government, which undertook to convert the dollar into gold at the rate of $35 per ounce. The dollar was thus literally as good as gold. This arrangement could be called the "dollar-gold standard." Governments participating in the Bretton Woods regime pledged to maintain their currencies' exchange rate vis-à-vis the dollar at an agreed-upon parity. However, when a country's economy was deemed to be in a fundamental disequilibrium that country could change the parity with the consent of the IMF. The exchange rate arrangement under the Bretton Woods regime could thus be said to have employed an "adjustable peg."

The Bretton Woods regime, in other words, was supported by two pillars. One was the dollar-gold standard and the other was the adjustable pegging of exchange rates. When President Nixon suspended the conversion of dollar into gold in August 1971, the first pillar of the regime collapsed. The dollar lost the guarantee of its value and became a mere national currency. When the major European countries and Japan agreed to float their currencies vis-à-vis the dollar in March 1973, the second pillar collapsed and the age of Bretton Woods ended.

Since the demise of the Bretton Woods regime the world has had no institutionalized global monetary arrangement. Indeed, it has had no system at all. In reality, as far as the choice of an international reserve and settlement currency is concerned, the world has moved slowly toward a multiple-currency regime. Although the foundation of the current regime is still what could be termed the "de facto dollar standard," the role of other currencies, such as the deutsche mark, the ECU, and the yen, has increased in importance. The fact that the dollar continues to be the key international currency in spite of the loss of the guarantee of its value can be explained by the still outstanding strength of the United States in many areas, including financial services. As to the exchange rate arrangement under the current "nonsystem," we may call it the "quasi-managed floating rate." Efforts are made frequently, at the national or multinational level, to manage the fluctuation of exchange rates in the market. So far, however, there have been few successful attempts and we still do not have any institutionalized method of management.

When we discuss international monetary arrangements in the twenty-first century with the hope of establishing a viable and effective arrangement, it is useful to look back on the performance of the Bretton Woods regime and the gold standard and identify the factors that made them so successful in their heydays. There were several common factors underlying their success. First, the United Kingdom and the United States enjoyed a hegemonic role in the global economic, political, and military arenas. They functioned as a stabilizing anchor in the management of global finance. Second, they maintained strong balance-of-payment positions. They did occasionally run trade deficits, but their current account balance was positive and therefore their position vis-à-vis creditors was strengthened. Third, the United Kingdom and United States, on the whole, followed sound economic policies conducive to sustainable noninflationary growth. In other words, owing to the foregoing three factors the pound sterling and the dollar could play the roles of key international currencies as cornerstones of the international monetary arrangement. Finally, countries other than the United Kingdom or the United States were convinced that it would be in their own best interests, from an economic as well as a political point of view, to comply with the international monetary arrangement under U.K. or U.S. leadership, even if such compliance placed certain constraints on their national autonomy.

The gold standard and the Bretton Woods regime functioned very well as long as the factors mentioned previously remained operative. When these factors ceased to apply, however, the arrangement itself became untenable. The decline in the leadership capabilities of the United Kingdom and the United States was the principal cause of the collapse of the global arrangement. When the Bretton Woods regime was functioning most successfully the United States' role as the guardian of the regime was solidified by the U.S. commitment to the open market and to maintaining a credible dollar. Today the United States is not reluctant to resort to talking down the dollar and to protectionism.

Prevailing conditions on the world economic scene today convince us that it is unrealistic to hope for the reestablishment of a global monetary arrangement like Bretton Woods. Major economic powers like the United States, Japan, and Germany are not willing to sacrifice such domestic economic objectives as growth, price stability, or fiscal soundness for the sake of exchange rate stability. In other words, there is no universal commitment to accept the symmetric obligation to correct a balance of payments disequilibrium. There is also no stable division of labor among major currencies. Since we do not have any single currency whose value is predominantly stable we cannot establish a reserve currency system that can be counted on by monetary authorities and market participants. Furthermore, compared with the 1950s and the 1960s, the volume of movable capital on a global scale has grown so enormously and its fluidity has increased so significantly that it would be utterly impossible for the authorities to control a mass capital movement once it started.

All in all, under the present circumstance of an international monetary framework that does not possess a stable center of gravity and the absence of a consensus about the mutual benefits of exchange rate stability, it is unlikely that major countries would be able to agree to institutionalize the international monetary arrangement, with its various disciplinary elements.

However, before we draw a final conclusion as to the feasibility of an institutionalized monetary arrangement it will be necessary to reflect on the importance of the stability of exchange rates. It is accepted wisdom that the lack of exchange rate stability is detrimental to the healthy expansion of trade and to investment, because the unpredictable fluctuation of exchange rates makes it difficult to ascertain the profitability of a deal. Historical data show that between the

Bretton Woods period and the post–Bretton Woods period the performance of the OECD economies deteriorated in terms of growth, trade, inflation, and employment. However, only further investigations will allow us to conclude to what extent the change in the international monetary arrangements, i.e., the loss of exchange rate stability, was responsible for this diminished economic performance.

It is reasonable to assume that for certain types of industries, particularly those producing internationally tradable goods, stability or predictability of exchange rates will certainly be welcome. Of course, even in that case the exchange rate should change, reflecting as it does a country's relative competitive position. Otherwise, an inflexible exchange rate may distort the optimum allocation of resources. Therefore, efforts to establish a viable and effective monetary arrangement must focus on the establishment of an arrangement that could help prevent too rapid or too volatile a fluctuation of exchange rates and help rectify prolonged misalignment, rather than the establishment of the arrangement that will ensure the least fluctuation of exchange rates. In other words, what we can and should aim for is a kind of "crisis management mechanism" to cope with deviations in the market that are inexplicable in terms of the underlying economic conditions in the countries concerned. We must accept those exchange rate fluctuations that reflect the changing dynamics of the underlying economic condition. To try to institutionalize exchange rate stability by putting in place an arrangement premised on the unconditional support of all the countries concerned would be totally unrealistic in today's environment.

What then should be done in order to make such a crisis management mechanism feasible? The most crucial condition for introducing stability into the international monetary situation is a common recognition among the major countries that they must pursue policies with a view to containing the domestic savings and investment imbalance, i.e., the external current account imbalance. Of course it is unrealistic to expect that all major countries can achieve a perfect account balance. But if they succeed in limiting the imbalance to, say, less than 2 percent of gross domestic production, they will have gone a long way toward promoting international monetary stability. An equally important condition is to convince the market that the appropriate authorities are not ignoring the imbalance. Indeed, even when there exists a considerable imbalance, if the market comes to realize that the authorities have a genuine willingness to correct it and have started to take the necessary measures to do so, the market tends to remain stable. When the environment has been prepared (as just described), the time will be ripe to begin designing a crisis management mechanism.

There is no question that coordination of macroeconomic policy among major countries is essential for the maintenance of a stable international monetary regime. Those who are skeptical about the prospects for the establishment of a viable international monetary arrangement try to justify their skepticism by pointing to the fact that no major countries are willing to sacrifice their immediate national interests for the sake of policy coordination. I certainly cannot disagree with them. Yet neither can I deny the possibility that acceptance of an international arrangement may have some disciplinary effect on a country's national policy formulation. The example of the Exchange Rate Mechanism, successful until its collapse in 1993, was a good example of the disciplinary effect of such an international arrangement. ERM was a success as long as member countries believed that the political and economic benefits of being a legitimate participant in such an international agreement more than offset the loss of some national autonomy. In other words there is a certain element of reciprocity. An international monetary arrangement will not be viable and effective unless members are willing to sacrifice a degree of national autonomy—but only when the arrangement is viewed as viable and effective will members support it at the expense of national autonomy.

If and when conditions are ripe for the design of a crisis management mechanism, I would propose one with the following principal features. A standing forum should be established within the organizational framework of the IMF. The forum would be chaired by the managing director of the IMF and would be made up of representatives of the major currency countries. For the sake of efficiency the number of participants should be kept to a minimum. At the same time it would be crucially important to have members of sufficiently senior stature that their recommendations could carry enough weight within their respective governments and central banks. The responsibility of the forum would be to monitor and assess the exchange market situation.

When the members of the forum detect disturbing developments in the market they would try to ascertain whether the situation represented a case of overshooting or of misalignment and thus required corrective action. If (no doubt with a great amount of luck) consensus is achieved on these points, the forum would ask the respective governments and central banks to take actions that could include macroeconomic measures or exchange market adjustments or both.

Although I fully understand the likely criticism that creating such a forum will be quite difficult in reality, I would argue that, if we really wish to achieve reasonable exchange market stability, then adoption of such a crisis management mechanism will be the most realistic approach.

References

Agenor, Pierre-Richard, Jagdeep S. Bhandari, and Robert P. Flood. 1992. "Speculative Attacks and Models of Balance of Payments Crises." *IMF Staff Papers* 39(June): 357–94.

Alesina, Alberto, Alessandro Prati, and Guido Tabellini. 1990. "Public Confidence and Debt Management: A Model and a Case Study of Italy." In *Public Debt Management: Theory and History,* edited by Rudiger Dornbusch and Mario Draghi, 94–118. Cambridge: Cambridge University Press.

Alogoskoufis, George S. 1993. "The Crisis in the European Monetary System and the Future of EMU." Birkbeck College, University of London.

Alogoskoufis, George S., and Ron Smith. 1991. "The Phillips Curve, the Persistence of Inflation, and the Lucas Critique: Evidence from Exchange-Rate Regimes." *American Economic Review* 81 (December): 1254–75.

Antolin, Pablo, and Olympia Bover. 1993. "Regional Migration in Spain: The Effect of Personal Characteristics and of Unemployment, Wage and House Price Differentials Using Pooled Cross Sections." Documento de Trabajo 9318, Servicio de Estudios, Banco de España.

Artis, M. J., and Mark P. Taylor. 1988. "Exchange Rates and the EMS: Assessing the Track Record." CEPR Discussion Paper 250. London: Centre for Economic Policy Research (April).

Atkeson, Andrew, and Tamim Bayoumi. 1991. "Do Private Capital Markets Insure against Risk in a Common Currency Area?" University of Chicago and International Monetary Fund.

Bank for International Settlements. 1992. *Recent Developments in International Interbank Relations.* Basel, Switzerland.

———. 1993. *Annual Report.*

Barro, Robert, and David Gordon. 1983. "Rules, Discretion and Reputation in a Model of Monetary Policy." *Journal of Monetary Economics* 12(July): 101–21.

Bayoumi, Tamim. 1990. "Saving-Investment Correlations: Immobile Capital, Government Policy, or Endogenous Behavior?" *IMF Staff Papers* 37(June): 360–87.

Bayoumi, Tamim, and Barry Eichengreen. 1992. "Is There a Conflict between EC Enlargement and European Monetary Unification?" Working Paper 3950. Cambridge, Mass.: National Bureau of Economic Research (January).

———. 1993. "Shocking Aspects of European Monetary Unification." In *Adjustment and Growth in the European Monetary Union,* edited by Francisco Torres and Francesco Giavazzi, 193–240. Cambridge University Press.

———. 1994a. "Monetary and Exchange Rate Arrangements for NAFTA." *Journal of Development Economics* 43 (February): 125–65.

———. 1994b. "The Political Economy of Fiscal Restrictions: Implications for Europe from the United States." *European Economic Review* 38: 783–91.

———. 1994c. "Macroeconomic Adjustment under Bretton Woods and the Post-Bretton Woods Float: An Impulse-Response Analysis." *Economic Journal* 104 (July): 813–27.

———. Forthcoming. "One Money or Many? On Analyzing the Prospects for Monetary Unification in Various Parts of the World." *Princeton Studies in International Finance.*

Bayoumi, Tamim, Morris Goldstein, and Geoffrey Woglom. 1994. "Do Credit Markets Discipline Sovereign Borrowers? Evidence from U.S. States." International Monetary Fund.

Bayoumi, Tamim, and Paul Masson. 1991. "Fiscal Flows in the United States and Canada: Lessons for Monetary Union in Europe." International Monetary Fund.

Begg, David, and Charles Wyplosz. 1993. "The European Monetary System: Recent Intellectual History." In *The Monetary Future of Europe.* London: Centre for Economic Policy Research.

Bennett, Adam G. G. 1993. "The Operation of the Estonian Currency Board." *IMF Staff Papers* 40 (June): 451–70.

Bergsten, C. Fred. 1993. "The Rationale for a Rosy View: What a Global Economy Will Look Like." *The Economist* 328(September): 57–59.

Bertola, Guiseppe. 1989. "Factor Mobility, Uncertainty and Exchange Rate Regimes." In *A European Central Bank? Perspectives on Monetary Unification after Ten Years of the EMS,* edited by Marcello de Cecco and Alberto Giovannini, 95–119. Cambridge University Press.

Bertola, Guiseppe, and Ricardo J. Caballero. 1990. "Target Zones and Realignments." Discussion Paper 398. London: Centre for Economic Policy Research (March).

Bertola, Guiseppe, and Lars E. O. Svensson. 1993. "Stochastic Devaluation Risk and the Empirical Fit of Target Zone Models." *Review of Economic Studies* 60 (July): 689–712.

Bini Smaghi, Lorenzo, and Silvia Vori. 1992. "Rating the EC as an Optimum Currency Area: Is It Worse than the United States?" In *Finance and the International Economy,* edited by Richard O'Brien, 78–92. Oxford University Press.

Blanchard, Olivier, Jean, and Lawrence F. Katz. 1992. "Regional Evolutions." *Brookings Papers on Economic Activity* 1: 1–66.

Blanchard, Olivier Jean, and Pierre Alain Muet. 1993. "Competitiveness through Disinflation: An Assessment of the French Macroeconomic Strategy." *Economic Policy: A European Forum* 16 (April): 11–56.

Blanchard, Olivier Jean, and Danny Quah. 1989. "The Dynamic Effects of Aggregate Demand and Supply Disturbances." *American Economic Review* 79 (September): 655–73.

Bloomfield, Arthur. 1959. *Monetary Policy under the International Gold Standard: 1880–1914.* Federal Reserve Bank of New York.

———. 1963. "Short-Term Capital Movements under the Pre-1914 Gold Standard." *Princeton Studies in International Finance* 11. International Finance Section, Department of Economics, Princeton University.

———. 1968. "Patterns of Fluctuation in International Investment before 1914." *Princeton Studies in International Finance* 21. International Finance Section, Department of Economics, Princeton University.

Bordo, Michael D. 1993a. "The Bretton Woods International Monetary System: A Historical Overview." In *A Retrospective on the Bretton Woods System,* edited by Michael D. Bordo and Barry Eichengreen, 3–108. University of Chicago Press.

———. 1993b. "The Gold Standard, Bretton Woods and Other Monetary Regimes: A Historical Appraisal." *Federal Reserve Bank of St. Louis Review* 75 (March–April): 123–91.

Bordo, Michael D., and Finn Kydland. 1992. "The Gold Standard as a Rule." Working Paper 9205. Federal Reserve Bank of Cleveland.

Borensztein, Eduardo, and Paul Masson. 1993. "Exchange Arrangements of Previously Centrally Planned Economies." In *Financial Sector Reforms and Exchange Arrangements in Eastern Europe,* edited by Guillermo A. Calvo and others, 29–56. IMF Occasional Paper 102. Washington, D.C.: International Monetary Fund (February).

Boughton, James M. 1992. "The CFA Franc: Zone of Fragile Stability in Africa." *Finance and Development* 29 (December): 34–36.

———. 1993. "The Economics of the CFA Franc Zone." In *Policy Issues in the Operation of Currency Unions,* edited by Paul R. Masson and Mark P. Taylor, 96–110. Cambridge University Press.

Branson, William. 1993. "The Unstable EMS: Comment." *Brookings Papers on Economic Activity* 1: 125–29.

Bruno, Michael. 1993. *Crisis, Stabilization and Economic Reform: Therapy by Consensus.* Oxford: Clarendon Press.

Bryant, Ralph C. Forthcoming. *International Coordination of National Stabilization Policies.* Integrating National Economies. Brookings.

Bryant, Ralph C., Peter Hooper, and Catherine Mann, eds. 1993. *Evaluating Policy Regimes.* Brookings.

Buiter, Willem, Giancarlo Corsetti, and Nouriel Roubini. 1993. "Excessive Deficits: Sense and Nonsense in the Treaty of Maastricht." *Economic Policy: A European Forum* 16 (April): 57–100.

Buiter, Willem H., and Jonathan Eaton. 1983. "International Balance of Payments Financing and Adjustment." In *International Money and Credit: The*

Policy Roles, edited by George M. von Furstenberg, 129–48. Washington, D.C.: International Monetary Fund.

Canzoneri, Matthew. 1985. "Monetary Policy Games and the Role of Private Information." *American Economic Review* 75 (December): 1056–70.

Canzoneri, Matthew, and Bizad Diba. 1991. "Fiscal Deficits, Financial Integration, and a Central Bank for Europe." *Journal of the Japanese and International Economies* 5 (December): 381–403.

Canzoneri, Matthew B., and Jo Anna Gray. 1985. "Monetary Policy Games and the Consequences of Noncooperative Behavior." *International Economic Review* 26 (October): 547–64.

Canzoneri, Matthew, B., and Carol Ann Rogers. 1990. "Is the European Community an Optimum Currency Area? Optimal Taxation versus the Cost of Multiple Currencies." *American Economic Review* 80 (June): 419–33.

Casella, Alessandra, and Jonathan Feinstein. 1989. "Management of a Common Currency." In *A European Central Bank? Perspectives on Monetary Unification after Ten Years of the EMS,* edited by Marcello de Cecco and Alberto Giovannini, 131–56. Cambridge University Press.

Chamie, Nick, Alain DeSerres, and Rene Lalonde. 1994. "Optimum Currency Areas and Shock Asymmetry: A Comparison of Europe and the United States." Working Paper 94-1. Bank of Canada (January).

Cohen, Benjamin. 1993. "Beyond EMU: The Problem of Sustainability." *Economics and Politics* 5 (July): 187–203.

Cohen, Daniel, and Charles Wyplosz. 1989. "The European Monetary Union: An Agnostic Evaluation." Discussion Paper 306. London: Centre for Economic Policy Research.

Collins, Susan, and Francesco Giavazzi. 1993. "Attitudes toward Inflation and the Viability of Fixed Exchange Rates: Evidence from the EMS." In *A Retrospective on the Bretton Woods System,* edited by Michael D. Bordo and Barry Eichengreen, 547–86. University of Chicago Press.

Commission of the European Communities. 1977. *Report of the Study Group on the Role of Public Finance in European Integration.* Luxembourg: Office for Official Publications of the European Communities.

Committee for the Study of Economic and Monetary Union (Delors Committee). 1989. *Report.* Luxembourg: Office for Official Publications of the European Communities.

Cooper, Richard. 1984. "A Monetary System for the Future." *Foreign Affairs* 63 (Fall): 166–84.

———. 1990. "What Future for the International Monetary System?" In *The Evolution of the International Monetary System,* edited by Yoshio Suzuki, Junichi Miyake, and Mitsuake Okabe, 277–300. University of Tokyo Press.

———. 1992. "Whither Europe?" *Yale Review* 80(July): 10–17.

Corden, W. Max. 1993. "Exchange Rate Policies for Developing Countries." *Economic Journal* 103 (January): 198–207.

Crockett, Andrew. 1994. "Monetary Implications of Increased Capital Flows." In *Changing Capital Markets: Implications for Monetary Policy,* 331–64. Federal Reserve Bank of Kansas City.

Cukierman, Alex, Miguel A. Kiguel, and Leonardo Leiderman. 1993. "The Choice of Exchange Rate Bands: Balancing Credibility and Flexibility." The Sackler Institute of Economic Studies, Tel Aviv University.

De Cecco, Marcello. 1984. *The International Gold Standard: Money and Empire,* 2d ed. London: Francis Pinter.

De Grauwe, Paul. 1993. "Real Convergence in a Monetary Union." University of Leuven.

De Kock, Gabriel, and Vittorio U. Grilli. 1989. "Endogenous Exchange Rate Regime Switches." Working Paper 3066. Cambridge, Mass.: National Bureau of Economic Research (August).

Deverajan, Shantayanan, and Dani Rodrik. 1991. "Do the Benefits of Fixed Exchange Rates Outweigh Their Costs? The Franc Zone in Africa." Working Paper 3727. Cambridge, Mass.: National Bureau of Economic Research (June).

Dominguez, Kathryn M., and Jeffrey A. Frankel. 1993. *Does Foreign Exchange Intervention Work?* Washington, D.C.: Institute for International Economics.

Dornbusch, Rudiger. 1987. "Exchange Rates and Prices." *American Economic Review* 77 (March): 93–106.

———. 1993. "The Unstable EMS: Comment." *Brookings Papers on Economic Activity* 1: 130–36.

Edison, Hali. 1993. "The Effectiveness of Central Bank Intervention: A Survey of the Post-1982 Literature." Special Papers in International Economics 18. International Finance Section, Department of Economics, Princeton University.

Edwards, Sebastian. 1992. "Exchange Rates as Nominal Anchors." Working Paper 4246. Cambridge, Mass.: National Bureau of Economic Research (December).

Eichenbaum, Martin, and Charles Evans. 1993. "Some Empirical Evidence on the Effects of Monetary Policy Shocks on Exchange Rates." Working Paper 4271. Cambridge, Mass.: National Bureau of Economic Research (February).

Eichengreen, Barry. 1991a. "The Comparative Performance of Fixed and Flexible Exchange-Rate Regimes: Interwar Evidence." In *Business Cycles: Theories, Evidence and Analysis,* edited by Niels Thygesen, Kumaraswamy Velupillai, and Stefano Zambelli, 229–72. London: Macmillan.

———. 1991b. "Trends and Cycles in Foreign Lending." In *Capital Flows in the World Economy,* edited by Horst Siebert, 3–28. Kiel Institute for World Economics.

———. 1992a. *Golden Fetters: The Gold Standard and the Great Depression, 1919– 1939.* Oxford University Press.

———. 1992b. "Should the Maastricht Treaty Be Saved?" *Princeton Studies in International Finance* 74, International Finance Section, Department of Economics, Princeton University (December).

———. 1993a. "Epilogue: Three Perspectives on the Bretton Woods System." In *A Retrospective on the Bretton Woods System,* edited by Michael D. Bordo and Barry Eichengreen, 621–58. University of Chicago Press.

———. 1993b. "A Payments Mechanism for the Former Soviet Union: Is the EPU a Relevant Precedent?" *Economic Policy: A European Forum* 17(October): 309–54.

————. 1993c. "Prerequisites for International Monetary Stability." Paper prepared for the Commission on the Future of the Bretton Woods Institutions. Working Paper C93-018. Center for International and Development Economies Research, University of California at Berkeley.

————. 1993d. "The Crisis in the EMS and the Transition to EMU: An Interim Assessment." In *Economic Policy Issues in Financial Integration,* edited by Seppo Honkapohja, 15–72. University of Helsinki.

————. Forthcoming. "The Endogeneity of Exchange Rate Regimes." In *Understanding Interdependence: The Macroeconomics of the Open Economy,* edited by Peter B. Kenen. Princeton University Press.

Eichengreen, Barry, and Jeffry Frieden. 1993. "The Political Economy of European Monetary Unification: An Analytical Introduction." *Economics and Politics* 5: 85–104.

Eichengreen, Barry, and Charles Wyplosz. 1993. "The Unstable EMS." *Brookings Papers on Economic Activity* 1: 51–124.

Emerson, Michael, and others. 1992. *One Market, One Money.* Oxford University Press.

Emminger, Otmar. 1986. *D-Mark, Dollar, Währungskrisen: Erinnerungen eines ehemaligen Bundes bank präsidenten.* Stuttgart: Deutsche Verlags-Anstalt.

Erlanger, Steven. 1994. "Russia and Belarus Agree to Unify Monetary Systems." *New York Times* (April 13): A6.

Fishlow, Albert. 1989. "Conditionality and Willingness to Pay: Some Parallels from the 1890s." In *The International Debt Crisis in Historical Perspective,* edited by Barry Eichengreen and Peter Lindert, 86–105. MIT Press.

Flood, Robert, and Peter Isard. 1989. "Monetary Policy Strategies." *IMF Staff Papers* 36(September): 612–32.

Flood, Robert, Andrew Rose, and Donald Mathieson. 1990. "An Empirical Exploration of Exchange Rate Target-Zones." Working Paper 3543. Cambridge, Mass.: National Bureau of Economic Research.

Flood, Robert P., and Peter M. Garber. 1984a. "Collapsing Exchange-Rate Regimes: Some Linear Examples." *Journal of International Economics* 17(August): 1–13.

————. 1984b. "Gold Monetization and Gold Discipline." *Journal of Political Economy* 92(February): 90–107.

Ford, A. G. 1962. *The Gold Standard, 1880–1914: Britain and Argentina.* Oxford: Clarendon Press.

Frankel, Jeffrey A. 1994. "Exchange Rate Policy." In *American Economic Policy in the 1980s,* edited by Martin Feldstein, 293–341. University of Chicago Press.

Frankel, Jeffrey A., and Kenneth Froot. 1988. "Chartists, Fundamentalists and the Demand for Dollars." In *Private Policy and Government Behavior in Interdependent Economies,* edited by T. Courakis and M. Taylor, 73–128. Oxford University Press.

Frankel, Jeffrey A., and Shang-Jin Wei. 1993. "Is There a Currency Bloc in the Pacific?" University of California at Berkeley.

Fratianni, Michele, and Jürgen von Hagen. 1992. *The European Monetary System and European Monetary Union.* Boulder: Westview Press.

Frenkel, Jacob A., Morris Goldstein, and Paul Masson. 1989. "Simulating the Effects of Some Simple Coordinated versus Uncoordinated Policy Rules." In *Macroeconomic Policies in an Interdependent World,* edited by Ralph Bryant and others, 202–59. Brookings.

Frieden, Jeffry. 1991. "Greenback, Gold and Silver: The Politics of American Exchange Rate Policy, 1870–1913." CIBER Working Paper 91-04. Anderson School of Management, University of California at Los Angeles (April).

Friedman, Milton. 1953. "The Case for Flexible Exchange Rates." In *Essays in Positive Economics,* 157–203. University of Chicago Press.

Friedman, Thomas L. 1994. "Fund is Set Up to Stabilize Mexican Peso." *New York Times* (April 27): D1, 18.

Froot, Kenneth, and Richard Thaler. 1990. "Anomalies: Foreign Exchange." *Journal of Economic Perspectives* 4 (Summer): 179–92.

Funabashi, Yoichi. 1988. *Managing the Dollar: From the Plaza to the Louvre.* Washington, D.C.: Institute for International Economics.

Gandolfo, Giancarlo. 1992. "Monetary Unions." In *The New Palgrave Dictionary of Money and Finance,* edited by Peter Neuman, Murray Milgate, and John Eatwell, 765–70. London: Macmillan.

Garber, Peter. 1993. "The Collapse of the Bretton Woods Fixed Exchange Rate System." In *A Retrospective on the Bretton Woods System,* edited by Michael D. Bordo and Barry Eichengreen, 461–94. University of Chicago Press.

Garber, Peter, and Vittorio Grilli. 1986. "The Belmont-Morgan Syndicate as an Optimal Investment Banking Contract," *European Economic Review* 30 (June): 649–77.

Garrett, Geoffrey. 1993. "The Politics of Maastricht." *Economics and Politics* 5 (July): 105–24.

Gavin, Michael. 1992. "Monetary Policy, Exchange Rates and Investment in a Keynesian Economy." *Journal of International Money and Finance* 11(April): 145–61.

Giavazzi, Francesco, and Alberto Giovannini. 1989. *Limiting Exchange Rate Flexibility: The European Monetary System.* MIT Press.

Giavazzi, Francesco, and Marco Pagano. 1990. "Confidence Crises and Public Debt Management." In *Public Debt Management: Theory and History,* edited by Rudiger Dornbusch and Mario Draghi, 125–43. Cambridge University Press.

Giovannini, Alberto. 1989. "How Do Fixed-Exchange-Rate Regimes Work? Evidence from the Gold Standard, Bretton Woods and the EMS." In *Blueprints for Exchange Rate Management,* edited by Marcus Miller, Barry Eichengreen, and Richard Portes, 13–42. New York: Academic Press.

———. 1991. "Is EMU Falling Apart?" *International Economic Outlook* 1 (June): 36–41.

———. 1992. "Economic and Monetary Union: What Happened? Exploring the Political Dimension of Optimum Currency Areas." In *The Monetary Future of Europe.* London: Centre for Economic Policy Research.

———. 1993. "Bretton Woods and Its Precursors: Rules versus Discretion in the History of International Monetary Regimes." In *A Retrospective on the Bretton*

Woods System, edited by Michael D. Bordo and Barry Eichengreen, 109–54. University of Chicago Press.

Goldstein, Morris, and others. 1993. *International Capital Markets: Part I. Exchange Rate Management and International Capital Flows.* Washington, D.C.: International Monetary Fund.

Goodhart, Charles. 1992. "Economic and Monetary Union (EMU) in Europe: A UK Perspective." In *Exchange-Rate Regimes and Currency Unions,* edited by Ernst Baltensperger and Hans-Werner Sinn, 183–99. St. Martin's Press.

———. Forthcoming. "The Political Economy of Monetary Union." In *Understanding Interdependence: The Macroeconomics of the Open Economy,* edited by Peter B. Kenen. Princeton University Press.

Gordon, James. 1991. "Structural Funds and the 1992 Program in the European Community." Working Paper WP/91/65. Washington, D.C.: IMF.

Goto, J., and Koichi Hamada. 1993. "Economic Preconditions for Asian Regional Integration." Discussion Paper 685. Yale Economic Growth Center.

Gros, Daniel, and Niels Thygesen. 1992. *European Monetary Integration.* St. Martin's. (Copyright ©1992 Daniel Gros and Niels Thygesen. Table 4-2 reprinted with permission of St. Martin's Press, Inc.)

Grossman, Herschel, and John van Huyck. 1988. "Sovereign Debt as a Contingent Claim: Excusable Default, Repudiation and Reputation." *American Economic Review* 78(December): 1088–97.

Group of Ten. 1993. "International Capital Movements and Foreign Exchange Markets: A Report to the Ministers and Governors by the Group of Deputies."

Hanke, Steve H., Lars Jonung, and Kurt Schuler. 1992. *Monetary Reform for a Free Estonia,* Stockholm: SNS Förlag.

Hansen, Lars Peter, and Robert J. Hodrick. 1980. "Forward Exchange Rates as Optimal Predictors of Future Spot Rates: An Econometric Analysis." *Journal of Political Economy* 88 (October): 828–53.

Hatton, T. J. 1988. "Institutional Change and Wage Rigidity in the UK, 1880–1985." *Oxford Review of Economic Policy* 4 (Spring): 74–86.

Havrylyshyn, Oleh, and John Williamson. 1991. *From Soviet Disunion to Eastern Economic Community,* Washington, D.C.: Institute for International Economics.

Hawtrey, R. G. 1913. *Good and Bad Trade.* London: Constable.

Honkapohja, Seppo, and Pentti Pikkarainen. 1992. "Country Characteristics and the Choice of Exchange Rate Regime: Are Mini-Skirts Followed by Maxis?" Discussion Paper 774. London: Centre for Economic Policy Research (December).

Horn, Henrik, and Torsten Persson. 1988. "Exchange Rate Policy, Wage Formation and Credibility." *European Economic Review* 32(October): 1621–36.

Hörngren, Lars, and Hans Lindberg. 1993. "The Struggle to Turn the Swedish Krona into a Hard Currency." Sveriges Riksbank.

Hugon, P., P. Cerruti, and S. Collignon. 1992. "Monetary Co-operation in Sub-Saharan Africa: The Role of Regional Settlements of Payments." In *Workshop on the Promotion of Regional Cooperation and Integration in Sub-Saharan Africa,* edited by European University Institute, 197–223. Florence: European University Institute.

Ingram, James C. 1959. "State and Regional Payments Mechanisms." *Quarterly Journal of Economics* 73(November): 619–32.

International Monetary Fund. Various years. *International Financial Statistics.* Washington, D.C.

Ishiyama, Yoshihide. 1975. "The Theory of Optimum Currency Areas: A Survey." *IMF Staff Papers* 22 (July): 344–83.

Italianer, Alexander, and Jean Pisani-Ferry. 1992. "Regional Stabilization Properties of Fiscal Arrangements: What Lessons for the Community?" Commission of the European Communities and CEPII.

Johnson, Harry G. 1970. "The Case for Flexible Exchange Rates, 1969," in *Approaches to Greater Flexibility of Exchange Rates,* edited by George N. Halm, 91–111. Princeton University Press.

Kaminsky, Graciela L., and Karen K. Lewis. 1993. "Does Foreign Exchange Intervention Signal Future Monetary Policy?" Working Paper 4298. Cambridge, Mass.: National Bureau of Economic Research (March).

Kenen, Peter B. 1969. "The Theory of Optimum Currency Areas: An Eclectic View." In *Monetary Problems of the International Economy,* edited by Robert A. Mundell and Alexander K. Swoboda, 41–60. University of Chicago Press.

———. 1988. *Managing Exchange Rates.* London: Royal Institute of International Affairs.

———. 1990. "The Coordination of Macroeconomic Policies." In *International Policy Coordination and Exchange Rate Fluctuations,* edited by William H. Branson, Jacob A. Frenkel, and Morris Goldstein, 68–108. University of Chicago Press.

———. 1992. *EMU after Maastricht.* Washington: Group of Thirty.

Kindleberger, Charles P. 1981. *International Money.* London: Allen and Unwin.

Krugman, Paul. 1979. "A Model of Balance-of-Payments Crises." *Journal of Money, Credit and Banking* 11 (August): 311–25.

———. 1990. "The Case for Stabilizing Exchange Rates." *Oxford Review of Economic Policy* 5 (Autumn): 61–72.

———. 1991. "Target Zones and Exchange Rate Dynamics." *Quarterly Journal of Economics* 51 (August): 669–82.

———. 1993. "Lessons of Massachusetts for EMU." In *Adjustment and Growth in the European Monetary Union,* Francisco Torres and Francesco Giavazzi, 241–69. Cambridge University Press.

Kydland, Finn E., and Edward C. Prescott. 1977. "Rules Rather than Discretion: The Inconsistency of Optimal Plans." *Journal of Political Economy* 85 (June): 473–92.

Lainela, Seija, and Pekka Sutela. 1993. "Escaping from the Rouble: Estonia and Latvia Compared." Bank of Finland.

Lewis, Karen K. 1990. "Occasional Interventions to Target Rates with a Foreign Exchange Application." Working Paper 3398. Cambridge, Mass.: National Bureau of Economic Research (July).

———. 1993. "Are Foreign Exchange Intervention and Monetary Policy Related and Does It Really Matter?" Working Paper 93–11. Weiss Center for International Financial Research, Wharton School.

McKinnon, R. I. 1963. "Optimum Currency Areas." *American Economic Review* 53 (September): 717–24.

McKinnon, Ronald I. 1990. "Interest Rate Volatility and Exchange Risk: New Rules for a Common Monetary Standard." *Contemporary Policy Issues* 8 (April): 1–17.

———. 1993. "The Rules of the Game: International Money in Historical Perspective." *Journal of Economic Literature* 31 (March): 1–44.

———. Forthcoming. "A Fiscally Consistent Proposal for Reforming the European Monetary System." In *Understanding Interdependence: The Macroeconomics of the Open Economy,* edited by Peter B. Kenen. Princeton University Press.

Mann, Catherine. 1986. "Prices, Profit Margins and Exchange Rates." *Federal Reserve Bulletin* (June): 366–79.

Martin, Lisa L. 1993. "International and Domestic Institutions in the EMU Process." *Economics and Politics* 5 (July): 125–44.

Mathieson, Donald J., and Liliana Rojas-Suárez. 1993. *Liberalization of the Capital Account: Experiences and Issues.* IMF Occasional Paper, 103. Washington, D.C.: International Monetary Fund (March).

Mencinger, Joze. 1993. "The Experience with the Tolar in Slovenia." University of Ljubijana. Paper presented at Centre for Economic Policy Research Conference on Economics of New Currencies, Frankfurt, June 28–29, 1993.

Miller, Marcus H. 1993. "The Break-up of the Ruble Zone and Prospects for a New Ukrainian Currency: A Monetary Analysis." University of Warwick. Paper presented at Centre for Economic Policy Research Conference on Economics of New Currencies, Frankfurt, June 28–29, 1993.

Mintz, Norman N. 1970. *Monetary Union and Economic Integration.* New York University Press.

Morgenstern, Oskar. 1959. *International Financial Transactions and Business Cycles.* Princeton University Press.

Mundell, R. A. 1961. "A Theory of Optimum Currency Areas." *American Economic Review* 51(September): 657–64.

Mundell, Robert. 1993. "EMU and the International Monetary System: A Transatlantic Perspective." Working Paper 13. Austrian National Bank.

Murphy, Robert. 1989. "Stock Prices, Real Exchange Rates and Optimal Capital Accumulation." *IMF Staff Papers* 36(March): 102–28.

Mussa, Michael. 1981. "The Role of Official Intervention." Occasional Papers 6. New York: Group of Thirty.

Mussa, Michael, and Morris Goldstein. 1994. "The Integration of World Capital Markets." In *Changing Capital Markets: Implications for Monetary Policy,* 245–314. Federal Reserve Bank of Kansas City: 245–314.

North, Douglass C. 1993. "Institutions and Credible Commitment." *Journal of Institutional and Theoretical Economics* 149(March): 11–23.

Obstfeld, Maurice. 1986. "Rational and Self-Fulfilling Balance-of-Payments Crises." *American Economic Review* 66(March): 72–81.

———. 1988. "The Effectiveness of Foreign-Exchange Intervention: Recent Experience." Working Paper 2796. Cambridge, Mass.: National Bureau of Economic Research (December).

———. 1991. "Destabilizing Effects of Exchange Rate-Escape Clauses." Working Paper 3603. Cambridge, Mass.: National Bureau of Economic Research (January).

———. 1993. "The Adjustment Mechanism." In *A Retrospective on the Bretton Woods System,* edited by Michael D. Bordo and Barry Eichengreen, 201–68. University of Chicago Press.

———. 1994. "The Logic of Currency Crises." Working Paper 4640. Cambridge, Mass.: National Bureau of Economic Research (February).

———. Forthcoming. "International Capital Mobility in the 1990s." In *Understanding Interdependence,* edited by Peter B. Kenen. Princeton University Press.

Organization for Economic Cooperation and Development. 1989. *Economies in Transition. Structural Adjustment in OECD Countries.* Paris.

Ozkan, F. Gulcin, and Alan Sutherland. 1994. "A Model of the ERM Crisis." Discussion Paper 879. London: Centre for Economic Policy Research (January).

Portes, Richard. 1993. "EMS and EMU after the Fall." *The World Economy* 16(January): 1–16.

Reichenbach, Horst, and others. 1993. "The Economics of Community Public Finance." *European Economy* (special issue) 5.

Repse, Einars. 1993. "The Experience with the Latvian Ruble and the Lats." Paper presented at Centre for Economic Policy Research Conference on Economics of New Currencies, Frankfurt, June 28–29.

Rogoff, Kenneth. 1984. "On the Effects of Sterilized Intervention: An Analysis of Weekly Data." *Journal of Monetary Economics* 14(September): 133–50.

———. 1985a. "The Optimal Degree of Commitment to an Intermediate Monetary Target." *Quarterly Journal of Economics* 100(November): 1169–89.

———. 1985b. "Can Exchange Rate Predictability Be Achieved without Monetary Convergence? Evidence from EMS." *European Economic Review* 28 (June–July): 93–115.

Sala-i-Martin, Xavier, and Jeffrey Sachs. 1992. "Federal Fiscal Policy and Optimum Currency Areas." In *Establishing a Central Bank: Issues in Europe and Lessons from the US,* edited by Matthew Canzoneri, Vittorio Grilli, and Paul Masson, 195–220. Cambridge University Press.

Schonfield, Andrew. 1965. *Modern Capitalism.* Oxford University Press.

Shiller, Robert J. 1989. *Market Volatility.* MIT Press.

Soros, George. 1987. *The Alchemy of Finance.* Simon & Schuster.

Stockman, Alan. 1987a. "The Equilibrium Approach to Exchange Rates." *Economic Review: Federal Reserve Bank of Richmond* 73 (March–April): 12–30.

———. 1987b. "Sectoral and National Aggregate Disturbances to Industrial Output in Seven European Countries." Working Paper 2313. Cambridge, Mass.: National Bureau of Economic Research (July).

Svensson, Lars E. O. 1992. "Why Exchange Rate Bands? Monetary Independence in Spite of Fixed Exchange Rates." Working Paper 4207. Cambridge, Mass.: National Bureau of Economic Research (November).

Takeda, M., and P. Turner. 1992. "The Liberalization of Japan's Financial Markets: Some Major Themes," BIS Economic Paper 34 (November).

Taylor, John. 1986. "An Econometric Evaluation of International Monetary Policy Rules: Fixed versus Flexible Exchange Rates." Stanford University.

Tollison, Robert D., and Thomas D. Willett. 1979. "An Economic Theory of Mutually Advantageous Issue Linkages in International Negotiations." *International Organization* 33 (Autumn): 425–49.

Tosini, Paula A. 1977. "Leaning against the Wind: A Standard for Managed Floating." *Princeton Essays in International Finance* 26, International Finance Section, Department of Economics, Princeton University (December).

Tower, Edward, and Thomas D. Willett. 1976. "The Theory of Optimum Currency Areas and Exchange-Rate Flexibility." *Princeton Special Papers in International Economics* 11, International Finance Section, Department of Economics, Princeton University (May).

Triffin, Robert. 1957. *Europe and the Money Muddle: From Bilateralism to Near-Convertibility, 1947–1956.* Yale University Press.

Ungerer, Horst, and others. 1986. "The European Monetary System: Recent Developments." Occasional Paper 48. Washington, D.C.: International Monetary Fund (December).

Vaubel, Roland. 1980. "The Return to the New European Monetary System: Objectives, Incentives, Perspectives." *Carnegie Rochester Conference Series on Public Policy* 13(Autumn): 173–222.

Weber, Axel. 1990. "EMU and Asymmetries and Adjustment Problems in the EMS: Some Empirical Evidence." Discussion Paper 448. London: Centre for Economic Policy Research (August).

West, Kenneth. 1987. "A Standard Monetary Model and the Variability of the Deutschemark-Dollar Exchange Rate." *Journal of International Economics* 23 (August): 57–76.

Williamson, John. 1985. *The Exchange Rate System,* revised ed. Policy Analyses in International Economics 5. Washington, D.C.: Institute for International Economics.

Williamson, John, and Marcus H. Miller. 1987. *Targets and Indicators: A Blueprint for the International Coordination of Economic Policy.* Policy Analyses in International Economics 22. Washington, D.C.: Institute for International Economics.

Woo, Wing T. 1985. "The Monetary Approach to Exchange Rate Determination under Rational Expectations: The Dollar–Deutschemark Rate." *Journal of International Economics* 15 (February): 1–16.

Yeager, Leland. 1966. *International Monetary Relations: Theory, History, and Policy.* Harper & Row.

Index